THE

Brendan Connell was born in Santa Fe, New Mexico, in 1970. His works of fiction include *The Architect* (PS Publishing, 2012), *Lives of Notorious Cooks* (Chômu Press, 2012), *Miss Homicide Plays the Flute* (Eibonvale Press, 2013), *Cannibals of West Papua* (Zagava, 2015), and *Against the Grain Again: The Further Adventures of Des Esseintes* (Tartarus Press, 2021). As editor he has worked on various projects, including *The Neo-Decadent Cookbook* (Eibonvale Press, 2020), which was co-edited by Justin Isis. As translator he has worked on various projects, including *Alcina and Other Stories* (Snuggly Books, 2019), by Guido Gozzano, which was co-translated by his wife Anna.

SNUGGLY BOOKS

THE WORLD IN VIOLET

An Anthology of
English Decadent Poetry

Edited and with an Introduction by
Brendan Connell

THIS IS A SNUGGLY BOOK

ISBN: 978-1-64525-080-7

CONTENTS

INTRODUCTION

Strictly speaking, the Decadent movement was a French movement, begun by Charles Baudelaire, his literary heirs, and disaffected Naturalists, such as J.-K. Huysmans, and eventually culminating in the work of writers such as Catulle Mendès, Jean Lorrain, Rachilde, and Renée Vivien. The influence of "the Decadents," however, was quickly felt throughout Europe and beyond, with the French movement being echoed, with varying levels of sonority, by writers and artists eager to imitate or display their own originality.

The Decadent literature of the British Isles and the United States, with which the present volume is principally concerned, was, for the most part, rather watered down in comparison with that of the Continent. On the one hand, the censors were more severe, but on the other, the Anglo Saxon mind-set was more apt to cling to the idea of morality in the arts, an idea that had been shunned by the best of the French writers for a generation or more. Oscar Wilde's *The Picture of Dorian Gray* seems exceedingly tame next to the work of Huysmans or Jean Lorrain, and the items published in *The Yellow Book*, that famous English Decadent journal, were more mild than what was being printed in the pages of many of the major daily newspapers of Paris, such as *Le Journal*, *La Lanterne*, and *Gil Blas*.

One area, however, where the English speakers seemed to live up to the full promise of the Decadent label, was in the realm of poetry. One would be hard-pressed indeed to find poetry more extreme and less morally bound than in certain pieces by George Moore, Vincent O'Sullivan or Aleister Crowley.

And though some of the names that will be found herein are quite well-known, it is likely that many will be new to all but the most devout connoisseurs. And so it should be.

The "minor poet" in conventional society is, generally speaking, looked upon as a creature to be pitied—the writer whose aspirations never led to success, never led to fame, and whose publications were altogether ignored or met with only rare praise or, if mentioned at all, were mentioned with despite. As far as Decadent poetry is concerned, however—at least as far as that written in the English language is concerned,—much of the "finest" work is that produced by these minor figures—drug addicts and suicides and those who lived their lives at the edges of social normalcy and found the ability to express themselves in small journals or volumes they self-published in editions so limited that few copies probably pierced beyond their circle of friends and acquaintances.

The current book therefore is, as much as anything, a tribute to those who, forgotten or remembered, often had tragic lives, and, even if they did not, were the impressionists of an age when the English language, having long lost its golden hue, still, sometimes, was able to glimmer in other shades—in violet shadows far, where the rose-red still lingered mid the grey.

✳

In compiling *The World in Violet*, I have occasionally asked for the thoughts or assistance of others. Foremost among these is Daniel Corrick, who I am indebted to for helping me acquire certain texts, some of the fruits of which can be found herein.

The order of the material is based on the birth year of the authors.

—Brendan Connell

THE WORLD IN VIOLET

ALGERNON CHARLES SWINBURNE

Satia Te Sanguine

If you loved me ever so little,
    I could bear the bonds that gall,
I could dream the bonds were brittle;
    You do not love me at all.

O beautiful lips, O bosom
    More white than the moon's and warm,
A sterile, a ruinous blossom
    Is blown your way in a storm.

As the lost white feverish limbs
    Of the Lesbian Sappho, adrift
In foam where the sea-weed swims,
    Swam loose for the streams to lift,

My heart swims blind in a sea
    That stuns me; swims to and fro,
And gathers to windward and lee
    Lamentation, and mourning, and woe.

A broken, an emptied boat,
    Sea saps it, winds blow apart,
Sick and adrift and afloat,
    The barren waif of a heart.

Where, when the gods would be cruel,
　Do they go for a torture? where
Plant thorns, set pain like a jewel?
　Ah, not in the flesh, not there!

The racks of earth and the rods
　Are weak as foam on the sands;
In the heart is the prey for gods,
　Who crucify hearts, not hands.

Mere pangs corrode and consume,
　Dead when life dies in the brain;
In the infinite spirit is room
　For the pulse of an infinite pain.

I wish you were dead, my dear;
　I would give you, had I to give
Some death too bitter to fear;
　It is better to die than live.

I wish you were stricken of thunder
　And burnt with a bright flame through,
Consumed and cloven in sunder,
　I dead at your feet like you.

If I could but know after all,
　I might cease to hunger and ache,
Though your heart were ever so small,
　If it were not a stone or a snake.

You are crueller, you that we love,
　Than hatred, hunger, or death;

You have eyes and breasts like a dove,
  And you kill men's hearts with a breath.

As plague in a poisonous city
  Insults and exults on her dead,
So you, when pallid for pity
  Comes love, and fawns to be fed.

As a tame beast writhes and wheedles,
  He fawns to be fed with wiles;
You carve him a cross of needles,
  And whet them sharp as your smiles.

He is patient of thorn and whip,
  He is dumb under axe or dart;
You suck with a sleepy red lip
  The wet red wounds in his heart.

You thrill as his pulses dwindle,
  You brighten and warm as he bleeds,
With insatiable eyes that kindle
  And insatiable mouth that feeds.

Your hands nailed love to the tree,
  You stript him, scourged him with rods,
And drowned him deep in the sea
  That hides the dead and their gods.

And for all this, die will he not;
  There is no man sees him but I;
You came and went and forgot;
  I hope he will some day die.

ADAH ISAACS MENKEN

Infelix

Where is the promise of my years;
    Once written on my brow?
Ere errors, agonies and fears
Brought with them all that speaks in tears,
Ere I had sunk beneath my peers;
    Where sleeps that promise now?

Naught lingers to redeem those hours,
    Still, still to memory sweet!
The flowers that bloomed in sunny bowers
Are withered all; and Evil towers
Supreme above her sister powers
    Of Sorrow and Deceit.

I look along the columned years,
    And see Life's riven fane,
Just where it fell, amid the jeers
Of scornful lips, whose mocking sneers,
For ever hiss within mine ears
    To break the sleep of pain.

I can but own my life is vain
    A desert void of peace;
I missed the goal I sought to gain,

I missed the measure of the strain
That lulls Fame's fever in the brain,
   And bids Earth's tumult cease.

Myself! alas for theme so poor
   A theme but rich in Fear;
I stand a wreck on Error's shore,
A spectre not within the door,
A houseless shadow evermore,
   An exile lingering here.

JOHN TODHUNTER

Euthanasia
(Fin de siècle)

Yes, this rich death were best:
Lay poison on thy lips, kiss me to sleep,
Or on the siren billow of thy breast
    Bring some voluptuous Lethe for life's pain,
        Some languorous nepenthe that will creep
          Drowsily from vein to vein;
        That slowly, drowsily, will steep
Sense after sense, till, down long gulfs of rest
    Whirled like a leaf, I sink to the lone deep.

It shall be afternoon,
And roses, roses breathing in the air!
Deliciously the splendour of deep June,
    Tempered through amber draperies, round us fall;
        And, like a dream of Titian, let thy hair
Bosom and arms glow all,
    Clouds of love's sunset, o'er me there:
    Kiss that last kiss; then low some golden tune
        Sing, for the dirge of our superb despair.

So let the clock tick on,
Measuring the soft pulsations of Time's wing,
While to the pulseless ocean, like a swan

Abandoned to an unrelenting stream,
　　Floating, I hear thee faint and fainter sing;
Till death athwart my dream
　　Shall glide, robed like a Magian king,
And ease with poppies of oblivion
　　This heart, the scorpion Life no more may sting.

JOHN ADDINGTON SYMONDS

A Portrait

Wide lucid eyes in cavernous orbits set,
 Aflame like living opals or the sea,
 Vibrant with floods of electricity,
 The soul projected in each fiery jet:
This thy fierce fascination haunts me yet;
 And I have dreamed all Venice into thee,
 Her domes of pearl, her heaven's immensity,
 And superhuman saints of Tintoret.
Hoarse-voiced art thou as Tritons of her brine;
 Swift as man-snaring murderous ocean shark;
 White as foam-wreaths brown over Lido's line;
Stealthy as bats that skim those waves at dark;
 Storm-browed with curls of thunder; leonine
 As the winged guardian war-beast of St Mark.

Wo Die Götter Night Sind, Walten Gespenster

Where gods are not, ghosts reign. When Phoebus fled
 Forth from his laurel-girt Parnassian shrine
 With hollow shriek, that shivering o'er the brine
 Thrilled through earth, air, the news that Pan was dead;
Dragons and demons reared their obscene head

From fanes oracular, fierce serpentine
Hissings, in lieu of Pythian runes divine,
Poured on the night perplexity and dread.
Thus, in the temple of man's mind, when faith,
Hope, love, affection, gods of hearth and home,
Have vanished; writhe dim sibilant desires,
Phantasmal superstitions, lust the wraith
And greed the vampire, sphinx-like fiends that roam
Through ruined brain-cells, ringed with fretful fire.

Love in Dreams

Love hath his poppy-wreath,
    Not Night alone.
I laid my head beneath
    Love's lilied throne:
Then to my sleep he brought
    This anodyne—
The flower of many a thought
    And fancy fine:
A form, a face, no more;
    Fairer than truth;
A dream from death's pale shore;
    The soul of youth:
A dream so dear, so deep,
    All dreams above,
That still I pray to sleep—
    Bring Love back, Love!

MATHILDE BLIND

A Winter Landscape

All night, all day, in dizzy, downward flight,
   Fell the wild-whirling, vague, chaotic snow,
   Till every landmark of the earth below,
Trees, moorlands, roads, and each familiar sight
Were blotted out by the bewildering white.
   And winds, now shrieking loud, now whimpering low,
   Seemed lamentations for the world-old woe
That death must swallow life, and darkness light.

But all at once the rack was blown away,
   The snowstorm hushing ended in a sigh;
   Then like a flame the crescent moon on high
Leaped forth among the planets; pure as they,
Earth vied in whiteness with the Milky Way:
   Herself a star beneath the starry sky.

The Forest Pool

Lost amid gloom and solitude,
A pool lies hidden in the wood,
A pool the autumn rain has made
Where flowers with their fair shadows played.

Bare as a beggar's board, the trees
Stand in the water to their knees;
The birds are mute, but far away
I hear a bloodhound's sullen bay.

Blue-eyed forget-me-nots that shook,
Kissed by a little laughing brook,
Kissed too by you with lips so red,
Float in the water drowned and dead.

DELAMERE FOREST.

Despair

Thy wings swoop darkening round my soul, Despair!
And on my brain thy shadow seems to brood
And hem me round with stifling solitude,
With chasms of vacuous bloom which are thy lair.
No light of human joy, no song or prayer,
Breaks ever on this chaos, all imbrued
With heart's-blood trickling from the multitude
Of sweet hopes slain, or agonising there.

Lo, wilt thou yield thyself to grief, and roll
Vanquished from thy high seat, imperial brain,
And abdicating turbulent life's control,
Be dragged a captive bound in sorrow's chain?
Nay! though my heart is breaking with its pain,
No pain on earth has power to crush my soul.

EUGENE LEE-HAMILTON

Strangled

There is a legend in some Spanish book
    About a noisy reveller who, at night,
    Returning home with others, saw a light
Shine from a window, and climbed up to look.
And saw within the room, hanged to a hook.
    His own self-strangled self, grim, rigid, white.
    And who, struck sober by that livid sight.
Feasting his eyes, in tongue-tied horror shook.

Has any man a fancy to peep in
    And see, as through a window, in the Past,
His nobler self, self-choked with coils of sin,
    Or sloth or folly? Round the throat whipped fast
The nooses give the face a stiffened grin.
    'Tis but thyself. Look well. Why be aghast?

Leonardo da Vinci to His Snakes
(1480)

I love to watch them, trickling on the floor,
    Like Evil's very oozings running free;
    Now livid blue, now green as green can be,
Now almost white, though black an hour before.

Their undulation, trammelled by no shore,
   Might be a ripple upon Horror's sea,
   The live meander moves so soundlessly,
Inscrutable as Magic's very core.

What if I painted a Medusa's head,
   Fresh severed, lying on its back, with brow
   Convulsed in death, and wan as moonlit lead;
And made the snakes, still writhing in a slow
   Death struggle round the temples that are dead,
Striving to quit them in a ceaseless flow?

Song of the Arrow-Poisoners

When nature was fashioned,
   The vapours of hell
Crept through to the surface,
   Insidious and fell.

Of plants that are deadly
   They fattened the root;
The sap of destruction
   Filled berry and fruit;

While trickles of horror,
   In numberless snakes,
Ran live through the grasses
   That summer awakes.

And tetanus followed
   The rattlesnake's grasp,

And palsy the ripple
Of cobra and asp.

The juice of creation
Is venom and blood,
And torture is master
Of earth and of flood.

All nature is teeming
With claw and with fang:
Above is the beauty,
Beneath is the pang.

In shadow and flowers
The leopardess lies;
Two living green embers
Glow wild in her eyes.

The sea is all sunshine;
The shark is beneath;
A wave of red water
Wells up from his teeth.

But man is the monarch
Of torture and death;
The breath of his nostrils
Is murder's own breath—

The hunter of hunters
Who hunts his own race,
Relentless and savage,
From off the earth's face.

So dip we the arrows
        In juices of night,
That madness and horror
        May follow their flight;

And waves, as of lava,
        May run in each vein,
Till lethargy deadens
        Unthinkable pain.

Baudelaire

A Paris gutter of the good old times,
        Black and putrescent in its stagnant bed,
        Save where the shamble oozings fringe it red,
Or scaffold trickles, or nocturnal crimes.

It holds dropped gold; dead flowers from tropic climes;
        Gems true and false, by midnight maskers shed;
        Old pots of rouge; old broken phials that spread
Vague fumes of musk, with fumes from slums and slimes.

And everywhere, as glows the set of day,
        There floats upon the winding fetid mire
The gorgeous iridescence of decay:

A wavy film of colour gold and fire
        Trembles all through it as you pick your way,
And streaks of purple that are straight from Tyre.

MICHAEL FIELD

La Gioconda

Leonardo Da Vinci
The Louvre

Historic, side-long, implicating eyes;
A smile of velvet's lustre on the cheek;
Calm lips the smile leads upward; hand that lies
Glowing and soft, the patience in its rest
Of cruelty that waits and does not seek
For prey; a dusky forehead and a breast
Where twilight touches ripeness amorously:
Behind her, crystal rocks, a sea and skies
Of evanescent blue on cloud and creek;
Landscape that shines suppressive of its zest
For those vicissitudes by which men die.

A Dance of Death

How lovely is a silver winter-day
    Of sturdy ice,
That clogs the hidden river's tiniest bay
    With diamond-stone of price
To make an empress cast her dazzling stones
    Upon its light as hail—
So little its effulgency condones

Her diamonds' denser trail
Of radiance on the air!
How strange this ice, so motionless and still,
Yet calling as with music to our feet,
So that they chafe and dare
Their swiftest motion to repeat
These harmonies of challenge, sounds that fill
The floor of ice, as the crystalline sphere
Around the heavens is filled with such a song
That, when they hear,
The stars, each in their heaven, are drawn along!

Oh, see, a dancer! One whose feet
Move on unshod with steel!
She is not skating fleet
On toe and heel,
But only tip-toe dances in a whirl,
A lovely dancing-girl,
Upon the frozen surface of the stream,
Without a wonder, it would seem,
She could not keep her sway,
The balance of her limbs
Sure on the musical, iced river-way
That sparkling, dims
Her trinkets as they swing, so high its sparks
Tingle the sun and scatter song like larks.

She dances 'mid the sumptuous whiteness set
Of winter's sunniest noon;
She dances as the sun-rays that forget
In winter sunset falleth soon
To sheer sunset:
She dances with a languor through the frost

As she never had lost,
In lands where there is snow,
The Orient's immeasurable glow.

Who is this dancer white?
      A creature slight,
Weaving the East upon a stream of ice,
      That in a trice
Might trip the dance and fling the dancer down?
Does she not know deeps under ice can drown?

This is Salome, in a western land,
An exile with Herodias, her mother,
      With Herod and Herodias:
And she has sought the river's icy mass,
      Companioned by no other,
To dance upon the ice—each hand
      Held, as a snow-bird's wings,
         In heavy poise.
Ecstatic, with no noise,
Athwart the ice her dream, her spell she flings;
And Winter in a rapture of delight
Flings up and down the spangles of her light.

Oh, hearken, hearken! . . . Ice and frost,
From these cajoling motions freed,
      Have straight given heed
To Will more firm: In their obedience
      Their masses dense
Are riven as by a sword. . . .
Where is the Vision by the snow adored?
      The Vision is no more
      Seen from the noontide shore.

Oh, fearful crash of thunder from the stream,
As there were thunder-clouds upon its wave!
        Could nothing save
The dancer in the noontide beam?
She is engulphed and all the dance is done.
        Bright leaps the noontide sun—
But stay, what leaps beneath it? A gold head,
That twinkles with its jewels bright
            As water-drops. . . .
O murdered Baptist of the severed head,
Her head was caught and girded tight,
And severed by the ice-brook sword, and sped
        In dance that never stops.
        It skims and hops
Across the ice that rasped it. Smooth and gay,
            And void of care,
        It takes its sunny way:
But underneath the golden hair,
And underneath those jewel-sparks,
            Keen noontide marks
A little face as gray as evening ice;
Lips, open in a scream no soul may hear,
Eyes fixed as they beheld the silver plate
That they at Macherontis once beheld;
While the hair trails, although so fleet and nice
The motion of the head is subjugate
To its own law: yet in the face what fear,
        To what excess compelled!

Salome's head is dancing on the bright
And silver ice. O holy John, how still
Was laid thy head upon the salver white,
        When thou hadst done God's will!

FRANCIS SALTUS SALTUS

Spleen

The nurse of my childhood was Pain,
  And my infant lips reveled and drank
From bare bosoms, consoling, humane,
  Milk sourer than hatreds, and rank,
   Till they dried by the drain,
   Till they withered and shrank.

And the foam of that milk's gangrene
  Was like oils to my parched tongue;
For right docile was I to wean
  As helpless my bodilet hung,
   Sucking pains that were keen,—
   Sucking pains till they stung!

When the torrent had ebbed in tide,
  The kindly, cold nipples I tore—
Into shreds, as I puled, and I cried
  Over flesh that was bleeding and sore,
   For more Pain from that side,
   For more Pain, and still more.

For the pleasures and joys of Pain
  Are as welcome, refreshing, and fresh
As the deluge of early spring rain,
  As the large-weighted drops to the flesh—

Of all kine, by murrain
Left skin-tender and nesh.

But I found no more Pain, while Spleen,
　　With its pale and its yellow leer,
With its infamous touch venene,
　　With its pitiless brutal sneer,
　　　　With its milt and its teen,
　　　　Came to blight my career.

A mantle of sinister gloom
　　Has made night of my light and day,
My vindictive thoughts shift and loom,
　　Vague fancies of Fear and Dismay,
　　　　While the spleens of the tomb
　　　　Suck my heart's blood away.

Souls of Flowers

See yon wondrous wild slumbrous red roses that fill
　　All the air with their rare rich perfume;
See each petal like metal that bendeth so still
In the dark shade of wood-glade and hill.
Will the white moon appear soon to thrill
　　All the trembling assembling grey torrents of gloom?

There are bright-rays and night-rays that revel in air,
　　To contend and to blend with the flowers;
The red roses in poses of fear and despair
Seem to shrink from the wink and the glare,
Of the Night's immense shadow's dense stare
　　And seem sighing and dying for moonlier powers.

So the muser, the chooser of beautiful things,
　　All the men born of ken and of thought;
Rose-like slumber and number each time the moon springs
Through the shrouds of Night's clouds, mist befraught,
Till its rays bless the phase of minds, taught,
　　Not to hate or to wait for the song that it sings.

And each chalice, flower-palace, is in my belief
　　But a hushed, fragrance-crushed poet's soul;
For when in bloom, its perfume pervades ev'ry leaf
For it longs for a song's sweet relief,
Being haunted, Night taunted by grief,
　　And it swayeth and prayeth for lights that condole.

Vulnerable

When unsymmetric chaos in its might
Ruled the dim, desolate earth and held it bare,
In gloomy caves there wandered everywhere
Amorphous monsters, larvae of affright,
Deep in the vast, impenetrable night,
They lived and loved, dreading no future care
Until their souls were fired to strange despair,
When God to dazzle them created light.
Groping like them through sin and ennui's gloom,
I lived in callous stupor strangely dumb;
Pleased with a changeless lot as dull time flies.
Oh pardoning woman in thy summer's bloom,
Why to illumine my dark soul did'st thou come,
To haunt me with the splendors of thine eyes!

THEO MARZIALS

Châtelard

A long day spent at Châtelard for sketching;
    A glowing sky above; another sky
As clear the lake beneath; towards it stretching
    The vines and long white walls where melons lie.

We set our easels in a small oasis
    Of orchard-shade, and wearied with the glare
Of noon, our eyes sought on each other's faces
    A rest in reading love, no secret there.

And in that love was nothing to remind us
    How we were leaving other things undone,
And Châtelard rose gloomily behind us,
    And cast a broad black shadow from the sun.

The chatty magpies whirl'd into the thickets,
    The deep datura's breath grew over-sweet.
The finches left their trilling to the crickets,
    The glow-worms glimmer'd faintly at our feet.

The yellowing tendrils quiver'd on the trestle,
    The night-wind found a word still to be said,
And made her heedless hands but closer nestle
    In mine—and yet the love was but half-read.

A long day spent for sketching!—Who'd discover
    A sketch in those unfinish'd shades and lines?
For now my heart alone can there recover
    The sense of glowing slopes and torrid vines.

O Châtelard! she left me when your orchard
    Grew cold and bare with Summer and the sun,
And death has left my heart all cleft and tortured,
    And stopp'd the loving ere the sketch was done.

A Tragedy

Death!
Plop.
The barges down in the river flop.
    Flop, plop,
  Above, beneath.
From the slimy branches the grey drips drop,
As they scraggle black on the thin grey sky,
Where the black cloud rack-hackles drizzle and fly
To the oozy waters, that lounge and flop
On the black scrag piles, where the loose cords plop,
As the raw wind whines in the thin tree-top.
    Plop, plop.
  And scudding by
The boatmen call out hoy! and hey!
And all is running in water and sky,
    And my head shrieks—"Stop,"
    And my heart shrieks—"Die."

My thought is running out of my head;
My love is running out of my heart;
My soul runs after, and leaves me as dead,
For my life runs after to catch them—and fled
They are all every one!—and I stand, and start,
At the water that oozes up, plop and plop,
On the barges that flop
        And dizzy me dead.
I might reel and drop.
        Plop
        Dead.

And the shrill wind whines in the thin tree-top.
        Flop, plop.

A curse on him.
        Ugh! yet I knew—I knew—
If a woman is false can a friend be true?
It was only a lie from beginning to end—
        My Devil—my "Friend"
I had trusted the whole of my living to!
        Ugh! and I knew!
        Ugh!
    So what do I care.
And my head is as empty as air—I can do,
        I can dare,

(Plop, plop,
The barges flop
Drip, drop.)
   I can dare, I can dare!
And let myself all run away with my head,
And stop.
         Drop
         Dead.
      Plop, flop.
            Plop.

GEORGE MOORE

A Sapphic Dream

I love the luminous poison of the moon,
The silence of illimitable seas,
Vast night, and all her myriad mysteries,
Perfumes that make the burdened senses swoon
And weaken will, large snakes who oscillate
Like lovely girls, immense exotic flowers,
And cats who purr through silk-enfestooned bowers
Where white-limbed women sleep in sumptuous state.

My soul e'er dreams, in such a dream as this is,
Visions of perfume, moonlight and the blisses
Of sexless love, and strange unreached kisses.

The Corpse

Wondering I gaze upon each lineament
Defaced by worms and swollen in decay,
And watch the rat-gnawed golden ringlets play
Around the sunken outline, shrivelled, bent
In hideous grimace. The bosom rent—
Is opening rose-like 'neath the sun's warm ray,
And nature, smiling on the new-born May,
Doth own this corpse a part of her intent.

I try to lift it from the ground, but lo!
The poor head falls. A locket thus detached
Lies in my hand; fear seizes hold on me,
I gaze upon it, trembling, for I know
The trinket well; one word thereon is scratched:
I read, and, bending, kiss her reverently.

Chez Moi

My white Angora cats are lying fast
Asleep, close curled together, and my snake,
My many-coloured Python, is awake,
Crawling about after a two-months' fast.

The parrot screams from time to time my last
Love's name; the atmosphere doth softly ache
With burning perfume, lazily I rake
And sift the smouldering embers of the past.

The women I have loved arise, and pass
Before me like the sun rays in a glass,
Alice and Lizzy, Iza and Juliette;
And some are blushing, some are pale as stone:
Heigho! The world spins in a circle yet . . .
My life has been a very pleasant one.

HORATIO F. BROWN

"Bored"
At a London Music

Two rows of foolish faces blent
In two blurred lines; the compliment,
The formal smile, the cultured air,
The sense of falseness everywhere.
Her ladyship superbly dressed—
    I liked their footman, John, the best.

The tired musicians' ruffled mien,
Their whispered talk behind the screen,
The frigid plaudits, quite confined
By fear of being unrefined.
His lordship's grave and courtly jest—
    I liked their footman, John, the best.

Remote I sat with shaded eyes,
Supreme attention in my guise,
And heard the whole laborious din,
Piano, 'cello, violin;
And so, perhaps, they hardly guessed
    I liked their footman, John, the best.

OSCAR WILDE

The Harlot's House

We caught the tread of dancing feet,
We loitered down the moonlit street,
And stopped beneath the harlot's house.

Inside, above the din and fray,
We heard the loud musicians play
The "Treues Liebes Herz" of Strauss.

Like strange mechanical grotesques,
Making fantastic arabesques,
The shadows raced across the blind.

We watched the ghostly dancers spin
To sound of horn and violin,
Like black leaves wheeling in the wind.

Like wire-pulled automatons,
Slim silhouetted skeletons
Went sidling through the slow quadrille.

They took each other by the hand,
And danced a stately saraband;
Their laughter echoed thin and shrill.

Sometimes a clockwork puppet pressed
A phantom lover to her breast,
Sometimes they seemed to try to sing.

Sometimes a horrible marionette
Came out, and smoked its cigarette
Upon the steps like a live thing.

Then, turning to my love, I said,
"The dead are dancing with the dead,
The dust is whirling with the dust."

But she—she heard the violin,
And left my side, and entered in:
Love passed into the house of lust.

Then suddenly the tune went false,
The dancers wearied of the waltz,
The shadows ceased to wheel and whirl.

And down the long and silent street,
The dawn, with silver-sandalled feet,
Crept like a frightened girl.

Un Amant de Nos Jours

The sin was mine; I did not understand;
   So now is music prisoned in her cave,
   Save where some ebbing desultory wave
Frets with its restless whirls this meagre strand.
And in the withered hollow of this land

Hath Summer dug herself so deep a grave,
That hardly can the leaden willow crave
One silver blossom from keen Winter's hand.

But who is this who cometh by the shore?
(Nay, love, look up and wonder!) Who is this
    That cometh in dyed garments from the South?
It is they new-found Lord, and he shall kiss
    The yet unravished roses of thy mouth,
And I shall weep and worship, as before.

Symphony in Yellow

An omnibus across the bridge
    Crawls like a yellow butterfly,
    And, here and there, a passer-by
Shows like a little restless midge.

Big barges full of yellow hay
    Are moored against the shadowy wharf,
    And, like a yellow silken scarf,
The thick fog hangs along the quay.

The yellow leaves begin to fade
    And flutter from the Temple elms,
    And at my feet the pale green Thames
Lies like a rod of rippled jade.

EDWARD CRACROFT LEFROY

Colores
A Moan after Moon-set

A parody of Mr. Swinbuurne's style as exemplified in
"Dolores"

O thou that art sanguine and subtle,
  With fingers so wicked and white,
And eyes that are black as a cuttle,
  And brows that are blue as a blight.
O terriblest torture invented!
  O purplest passion intense!
(Have you heard of a poet demented,
  Benign Common-sense?)

O love that is redder than roses!
  O hate that is whiter than snow!
That blinkedly blindedly blazes,
  When black-blooded blast-blisses blow;
Desert us, disdain us, O never!
  Still fashion our fatuous fate;
O lick us and kick us for ever,
  Red love and white hate!

Let thy crying out-crimson the poppy,
  Thy yellings out-yellow the moon
All gilt with the gold of her copy

While thy moanings are Simply maroon;
Let the robe of thy redness be rounded,
    And the doom of desire be dense;
(Let the meaning of this be expounded,
    Say I, Common-sense.)

By the foam and the froth and the flashes,
    The flashes, the froth and the foam,
By the crag-cradled craving and crashes
    Through globulous glimmering gloom,
By the red, by the redder, the reddest,
    The greenest, the greener, the green,
By the folly that feeds where thou feddest,
    And licks thy plate clean.

By the fin-smashing fists that have smitten
    The bruises that blacken and bud,
By the tawny-tailed cur that has bitten
    When the thong has come down with a thud,
By all that is cruel and crimson,
    By all that is mean and immense,
(In a word, by the horrors he hymns on,
    Benign Common-sense.)

Who shall say whether red is ecstatic,
    Or green a more furious hue?
Must it always remain problematic
    Whether passion is purple or blue?
Sea-serpents sequestered in sadness,
    That satiate sorrow with salt,
O read us this riddle of madness,
    Since we are at fault!

So the saffron shall simulate sable,
    The bluest and blackest shall blend,
All the bases shall build them a Babel,
    Red, blue, green,—and so on to the end.
(Ye bards that make Bedlam your model,
    Remove your absurdities hence!
Come down and redeem us from twaddle,
    Benign Common-sense!)

OXFORD, 1876.

Quem Di Diligunt

O kiss the almond-blossom on the rod!
A thing has gone from us that could not stay.
At least our sad eyes shall not see one day
All baseness treading where all beauty trod.
O kiss the almond-blossom on the rod!
For this our budding Hope is caught away
From growth that is not other than decay
To bloom eternal in the halls of God.
And though of subtler grace we saw no sign,
No glimmer from the yet unrisen star,
Full-orbed he broke upon the choir divine,
Saint among saints beyond the golden bar,
Round whose pale brows new lights of glory shine—
The aureoles that were not and that are.

A Football Player

If I could paint you, friend, as you stand there,
Guard of the goal, defensive, open-eyed,

Watching the tortured bladder slide and glide
Under the twinkling feet; arms bare, head bare,
The breeze a-tremble through crow-tufts of hair;
Red-brown in face, and ruddier having spied
A wily foeman breaking from the side;
Aware of him,—of all else unaware:
If I could limn you, as you leap and fling
Your weight against his passage, like a wall;
Clutch him, and collar him, and rudely cling
For one brief moment till he falls—you fall:
My sketch would have what Art can never give—
Sinew and breath and body; it would live.

Dream-Travel

At night on Fancy's moon-lit main
I launch my shallop, like a thief
From doom of Justice fugitive,
If haply I may glide and gain
The land whereof sad hearts are fain,
Where lotos hangs a heavy leaf,
And amaranth is grown for grief,
For grief that is no longer pain;
And human tongues are like a tune
Heard faintly through the dusk of June,
As though in some unearthly grot,
Where Fate and Force and Fear are not,
A silver-throated choir did sing
To softest note of pshawm-playing.

PERCY EDWARD PINKERTON

Auto-da-Fé

Dead sinners stain the sunset
That flames above yon wood;
God burns them in His braziers,
And revels in their blood.
Yet 'twere delicious pleasure
The west to incarnadine,
That so your eyes, my darling,
Might once more look in mine.

Mors Pronuba

Dark sepulchres would lose their gloom
    If close to me
You couched resplendent in my tomb
    Where none could see;
The sordid world that throbbed above
Should have no part in our great love.

Tremendous torches in the dark
    Would be those eyes,
As all your soft, white body stark
    Became my prize,
As under asphodels and weeds
We wrought our warm, delirious deeds.

No archangelic summons then
　　　Might rouse our fears;
No Michael trumpeting to men
　　　Across the spheres
　Should balk us of this ritual rare
　As, lip on lip, we wrestled there.

The Shrine

　　Within a wood I wrought
　　In Passion's praise a shrine;
　　And as oblation brought
　　Red blossoms, amber wine,
　　That so I might appease
　　The ruthless god with these.

　　And gazing thro' the boughs
　　With grave, appealing eyes,
　　A young faun heard my vows
　　In reverent surprise;
　　Intent perchance to guess
　　The cause of my distress.

　　Then, with resistless charm
　　To me did he incline:
　　Encircled by his arm,
　　I felt his lips touch mine:
　　They made my spirit to be
　　At one with wind and tree.

So with him now I share
Sweet Nature's subtle moods:
The secrets of the air,
The music of the woods:
Red Passion's trophies rust:
The shrine I made is dust.

WILLIAM SHARP

A Paris Nocturne

Over the lonesome hollows
And secret haunts of the river,
Past fields and homestead and village,
Past the grey wharves and the piers
The darkness moves like a veil,
Save when obscure, vast, nigrescent
Flakes from the travelling gloom
Slant westward great fans of blackness.

Then a mist of radiance,
Lamps with red lights and yellow,
Foam-white, and blue as an ice-floe,
Lamps intermingling with gas-light,
Leagues of wind-wavered gas-light,
Lamps on the masts of barges,
Lamps upon sloops and on steamers,
Lamps below quays and dark bridges
Yellow and red and green,
Like a myriad growths phosphorescent
When a swamp, erewhile flooded with waters,
Lies low to the stare of the moon
And the stealthy white breath of the wind.

And, over all, one light
Palpitant, circular, wide,
Sweeping the city vast—
Yonder, beyond where in shadow
The thronged Champs-Elysées are filling
With echoes of human voices,
With shadows of human lives,
With phantoms of vampyre-vices—
Beyond where the serpentine river
Curves in a coil gigantic,
And straight, a thin shaft, through the vagueness
Soars the high lighthouse of Paris,
Soars o'er the sea of the city
With all its shoals and its terrors,
Its perilous straits and its breakers,
High o'er the brightness and splendour
Of shores where the sirens sing ever.

Then, shadows enmassed once again
And the river moving slowly,
And the hills making darkness deeper.
The lamps now fewer and fewer—
Fewer the red lights and yellow,
Till only a dusky barge
Moves like a water-snake
On the face of a dark lagoon,
A stealthy fire 'mid the stillness
While from a weir in the distance
Comes a sound like the cry of waters
When the tides and the sea-winds gather
And the sands of the dunes are scattered
In the scud of the spray.

An Untold Story

I.

When the dark falls, and as a single star
The orient planets blend in one white ray
A-quiver through the violet shadows far
Where the rose-red still lingers mid the grey:

And when the moon, half-cirque arm around her hollow,
Casts on the upland pastures shimmer of green:
And the marsh-meteors the frail lightnings follow,
And wave laps into wave with amber sheen—

O then my heart is full of thee, who never
From out thy beautiful mysterious eyes
Givest one glance at this my wild endeavour,
Who hast no heed, no heed, of all my sighs:

Is it so well with thee in thy high place
That thou canst mock me thus even to my face?

II.

Dull ash-grey frost upon the black-grey fields:
Thick wreaths of tortured smoke above the town:
The chill impervious fog no foothold yields,
But onward draws its shroud of yellow brown.

No star can pierce the gloom, no moon dispart:
And I am lonely here, and scarcely know

What mockery is "death from a broken heart,"
What tragic pity in the one word: Woe.

But I am free of thee, at least, yea free!
No more thy bondager 'twixt heaven and hell!
No more there numbs, no more there shroudeth me
The paralysing horror of thy spell:

No more win'st thou this last frail worshipping breath,
For twice dead he who dies this second death.

EDGAR SALTUS

Akosmism

As one who to some long-locked chamber goes,
    And listens there to what the dead have said,
    So there are moments when my thoughts are led
To those dull chronicles whose pages close
Epochs and ages in the same repose
    That shall the future as the past o'erspread,
    And where but Memory may tend the dead,
Or prune the ivy where once grew the rose.
    And as there to me from their pages streams
    The incoherent story of the years,
The aimlessness of all we undertake,
    I think our lives are surely but the dreams
    Of spirits dwelling in the distant spheres,
Who, as we die, do one by one awake.

Imeros

My heart a haunted manor is, where Time
    Has tumbled noiselessly with mouldering hands:
    At sunset ghosts troop out in sudden bands,
At noon 'tis vacant as a house of crime:

But when, unseen as sound, the night-winds climb
  The higher keys with their unstilled demands,
  It wakes to memories of other lands,
And thrills with echoes of enchanted rhyme.

Then, through the dreams and hopes of earlier years,
  A fall of phantom footsteps on the stair
    Approaches near, and ever nearer yet.
A voice rings through my life's deserted ways:
  I turn to greet thee, Love. The empty air
    Holds but the spectre of my own regret.

Poppies and Mandragora

My soul is full of linnets, my life is full of light,
For home, I have the mirage of a garden of delight.

My soul is full of tulips, my life is full of song.
For food I have the visions, that about a poet throng.

My soul is full of rainbows, my life is filled with love.
For wine I have the beauty of the stellar fields above.

Also, my heart is leaden, fear nails me on the rack.
My dreams are dreams of torture and my days are
  draped in black.

My soul is sick with horror, my life is drenched with care,
Morphine I have for portion, and I have, for bride,
  despair.

JOHN DAVIDSON

Holiday

Lithe and listen, gentlemen:
Other knight of sword or pen
Shall not, while the planets shine,
Spend a holiday like mine:—

Fate and I, we played at dice:
    Thrice I won and lost the main;
Thrice I died the death, and thrice
    By my will I lived again.

First, a woman broke my heart,
    As a careless woman can,
Ere the aureoles depart
    From the woman and the man.

Dead of love, I found a tomb
    Anywhere: beneath, above,
Worms nor stars transpierced the gloom
    Of the sepulchre of love.

Wine-cups were the charnel-lights;
    Festal songs, the funeral dole;
Joyful ladies, gallant knights.
    Comrades of my buried soul.

Tired to death of lying dead
    In a common sepulchre,
On an Easter morn I sped
    Upward where the world's astir.

Soon I gathered wealth and friends;
    Donned the livery of the hour;
And atoning diverse ends
    Bridged the gulf to place and power.

All the brilliances of Hell
    Crushed by me, with honeyed breath
Fawned upon me till I fell,
    By pretenders done to death.

Buried in an outland tract,
    Long I rotted in the mould,
Though the virgin woodland lacked
    Nothing of the age of gold.

Roses spiced the dews and damps
    Nightly falling of decay;
Dawn and sunset lit the lamps
    Where entombed I deeply lay.

My Companions of the Grave
    Were the flowers, the growing grass;
Larks intoned a morning stave;
    Nightingales, a midnight mass.

But at me, effete and dead,
　　Did my spirit gibe and scoff:
Then the gravecloth from my head,
　　And my shroud—I shook them off!

Drawing strength and subtle craft
　　Out of ruin's husk and core,
Through the earth I ran a shaft
　　Upward to the light once more.

Soon I made me wealth and friends;
　　Donned the livery of the age;
And atoning many ends
　　Reigned as sovereign, priest, and mage.

But my pomp and towering state,
　　Puissance and supreme device
Crumbled on the cast of Fate—
　　Fate, that plays with loaded dice.

I whose arms had harried Hell
　　Naked faced a heavenly host:
Carved with countless wounds I fell,
　　Sadly yielding up the ghost.

In a burning mountain thrown
　　(Titans such a tomb attain)
Many a grisly age had flown
　　Ere I rose and lived again.

Parched and charred I lay; my cries
　　Shook and rent the mountain-side;

Lustres, decades, centuries
   Fled while daily there I died.

But my essence and intent
   Ripened in the smelting fire:
Flame became my element;
   Agony, my soul's desire.

Twenty centuries of Pain,
   Mightier than Love or Art,
Woke the meaning in my brain
   And the purpose of my heart.

Straightway then aloft I swam
   Through the mountain's sulphurous sty:
Not eternal death could damn
   Such a hardy soul as I.

From the mountain's burning crest
   Like a god I come again,
And with an immortal zest
   Challenge Fate to throw the main.

CHARLES KAINS JACKSON

Impressions

In White

The morning light was on the bed
   Sheer silver laid on silver grey,
The sudden subtle dawn was shed
   In argent fire, and night was day;
   I rose and looked across the bay.
What morn will bring my love to me?
   Ah, life is love and life is gay,
White sails upon a silver sea!

In Rose-Pink

No more alone, but night is o'er
   And to the beach our way we make
And strip on the familiar shore
   While all the summer birds, awake.
   The inland woods with music shake.
Sing birds, while rapt I gaze upon
   Those glowing limbs, those lips which take
Love's rose-pink and vermilion.

In Violet

The purple mystery of night
    Once more upon the land descends,
And flaming sunset yields to light
    Where blue with red in music blends.
    The colour consecrate to friends.
The colour when the sun has set.
    The line wherewith the vision ends
The secret of the violet.

Lysis Aged XIII

Elos purissimi amoris
Et amoeni Bos pudoris
Atque ridens ac jocundus
Solem amans, floribundus
Puer vultûs gracilis,
Osculandis oculis;
How the Monks of old had written
By the Higher Beauty smitten,
Had they lived to gaze on you
They had known what Plato knew
And had praised what he divines,
In less imperfect leonines.

DOLLIE RADFORD

A Novice

What is it, in these latter days,
Transfigures my domestic ways,
And round me, as a halo, plays?
       My cigarette.

For me so daintily prepared,
No modern skill, or perfume, spared,
What would have happened had I dared
       To pass it yet?

What else could lighten times of woe,
When some one says "I told you so,"
When all the servants, in a row,
       Give notices?

When the great family affairs
Demand the most gigantic cares,
And one is very ill upstairs,
       With poultices?

What else could ease my aching head,
When, though I long to be in bed,
I settle steadily instead
       To my "accounts?"

And while the house is slumbering,
Go over them like anything,
And find them ever varying,
        In their amounts!

Ah yes, the cook may spoil the broth,
The cream of life resolve to froth,
I cannot now, though very wroth,
        Distracted be;

For as the smoke curls blue and thin
From my own lips, I first begin
To bathe my tired spirit in
        Philosophy.

And sweetest healing on her pours,
Once more into the world she soars,
And sees it full of open doors,
        And helping hands.

In spite of those who, knocking, stay
At sullen portals day by day,
And weary at the long delay
        To their demands.

The promised epoch, like a star,
Shines very bright and very far,
But nothing shall its lustre mar,
        Though distant yet.

If I, in vain, must sit and wait,
To realize our future state,
I shall not be disconsolate,
        My cigarette!

HENRY WILLARD AUSTIN

Une Fleur du Mal

She found a flower by the wayside—
  A wonderful, white flower;
    But evil was the hour
She lifted it from the wayside
  And brought it to her bower.

For there it grew gigantic,
  A coiling colonnade
  Like to the banyan's shade;
And, like a snake gigantic,
  Its tendrils round her played.

And its blossoms so white—ah! cruel—
  To a frosty silver turned
  And their quivering edges burned
From that to a crimson as cruel
  As ever 'mid flames discerned.

And it breathed a poisonous odor
  Which was hot by fits and starts;
  Then cold, as the icy darts
That Winter throws—an odor
  Which entered her heart of hearts.

So the Woman lay dead, or dreamed it;
    And that Flower of frost and fire
    Became her funeral pyre;
Poor Heart, who Love had dreamed it,
    When it only was Desire!

HAVELOCK ELLIS

Schubert's Symphony in B Minor

I shudder at the awful airs that flow
    Across my soul; I hear crushed hopes that wail
    And flutter their brief wings and sudden fail—
Wild tender cries that sing and dance and go
In wonderful sweet troops. I cannot know
    What rends within my soul what unseen veil,
    And tells anew what strangely well-known tale
Of infinite gladness and of infinite woe.

Was I long since thrust forth from Heaven's door,
    Where in that music I had borne my part?
Or had this symphony its birth before
    The pulse of nature turned to laws of art?
O what familiar voice, from what far shore,
    Calls to a voice that answers in my heart!

COUNT ERIC STENBOCK

The Song of the Unwept Tear

I dreamed a dreadful dream, almost
  Too terrible to tell;
I dreamed that you and I, my love,
  Together were in Hell.

I dreamed in all eternity
  We two together were;
Condemned each other's face and limbs
  In hate and rage to tear.

I dreamed your kisses keen, my love,
  Bit my flesh through and through;
I tasted the salt taste of blood,
  My love, as I kissed you.

I dreamed your soft warm limbs, my love,
  Burnt with Hell's furious fire;
And demons laughed, and said, This is
  The end of your desire.

Think'st thou they weep with many tears,
  Deem'st thou their brows are knit with pain?
Ah no! far worse than that, they laugh—
  Their laugh is hollow and insane.

Almost too horrible to hear,
    Too terrible to tell,
The song about the unwept tear,
    And the laughter heard in Hell.

The Lunatic Lover

Ah, love, I dreamed of thee last night,
    Of strange lips kissing me,
With subtle penetrating pain—
    A moon veil shrouded thee
(I shudder, when I think of this,
    That a moon veil shrouded thee);
Thine eyes had in them all the light
    Of the moonlight on the sea.

Thine eyes are beautiful and soft,
    As the eyes of Seraphim,—
Ah, limpid liquid lustrous eyes,
    Sad eyes half bright, half dim,
Half without light, half brighter bright,
    Than the eyes of Seraphim.

That strange magnetic glance, that gleams
    From those mystic eyes of vair,
That face so brilliantly pale,
    And yet withal so fair,—
Love-pale and passion-pale, and yet,
    So marvellously fair,—

That countenance corpse-like refined,
    And subtle coloured hair.

Thy slender limbs that seem to burn
    Thy vesture through with fire,
That serpentine electric form
    Half quivering with desire,
Thy movements full of grace divine
    As the music of the lyre—
(Alas! for whoso looks on thee
    Feels new and strange desire,
The serpent winds around his heart,
    His soul is turned to fire,
As though within his veins there ran
    A current of Hell fire.)

I know, I know that long ago
    The moon with silver feet
Crept to thy bed, close to thine head,
    And kissed thy forehead, sweet,
Giving thy lips strange wine to drink,
    And alien flesh to eat,
And apples culled from the Dead Sea,
    Which are the serpent's meat,
Fruit from the tree by the Dead Sea
    Whose fruit is death to eat.

Note. —We have deemed it more judicious to represent the
rest of this poem by ********.

                             —S.E.S.

The Death-Watch

Darling, would you be sorry
   If you knew that I were dead?
Who loved you above all things,
   Though never word I said.

Did you know dear, that I loved you?
   One day your look was kind,
And one day—oh, so sad, love!
   Were I dead, dear, would you mind?

Eyes! that I dared not look to,
   Lips I that I dared not touch—
Would you pray for me a little,
   Who prayed for you so much?

If passing to my grave, dear,
   On some sad All Souls day—
Oh! where your tears had fallen
   Violets would bloom alway.

FREDERICK ROLFE

Sonnet (After the manner of C.J.R. Esquire): Of Gore

Upon night's violet vivid verge was lain
 The Horoscope of Time. Of sacrificial fowls
 A gaunt gray grizzly bear bore blood red bowels.
While dark dank weeds swang twisted twice or twain
And still the giant groaned in grievous pain.
 And still or ghoulish gasps or ghastly growls
 Burst bubbling forth, cheeks (so to speak) by jowls.
When suddenly the moon began to wane,—
Began to wane,—and down the bulging bank
 That slimy visage slid with staring eyes,
  Slid swifter till the dev'lish deed was done.
The mouldering corse plunged in the pool and sank!
 Ah Hell!! Five flaming Furies round me rise!!!
  And hist!!!! The thud o' the blood-drops one by one!!!!!

Sonnet: A Victim

Mark well one lonely Mortal amid a Sea
 Of scandalous Scorn, where Spite doth hiss and groan,
 Whose Waves are Friends who cast the ready Stone
To win some anguished Gasp of Agony:
(So young Sebastian chose his Weird to dree:)

Deaf to their venomed Rage, he cares for none
Of those who stab because he stands alone:
For, of that Door of Gold, he hath the Key,
    Where, all unshamed because the Saints are there,
    (Where God's eternal Gardens gleam and glow,)
    Sebastian's stainless Soul no Soil doth know,
The radiant Glory of his Youth to bare,
    And light the Land, where fadeless lilies blow,
With his Limbs of flaming Whiteness and rayed Hair.

JOHN BARLAS

Oblivion

Oblivion! is it not one name of death?
    Nay, is not Lethe death's most dismal name,
    Death growing hour by hour within our frame,
Death settling slowly in our brain, the breath
Of the soul ebbing, so that he who saith,
    I am to-day as yesterday the same,
    Lies, for his thoughts are fled like smoke from flame,
And like the dew his sorrow vanisheth.
Changed is the river, though the waves remain,
    Which rocks of slowlier-changing circumstance
        Plough up in every day of chafing foam.
Changed is the river, gone, gone to the main,
    Yesterday's dream and last year's happy chance,
        And the heart's thoughts again return not home.

Beauty's Anadems

A dagger-hilt crusted with flaming gems:
A queen's rich girdle clasped with tiger's claws;
A lady's glove or a cat's velvet paws;
The whisper of a judge when he condemns;
Fierce night-shade berries purple on their stems
Among the rose's healthsome scarlet haws;

A rainbow-sheathed snake with jagged jaws:
Such are queen Beauty's sovran anadems.
For she caresses with a poisoned hand,
And venom hangs about her moistened lips,
And plots of murder lurk with her eyes
She loves lewd girls dancing a saraband
The murderer stabbing till all his body drips,
And thee, my gentle lady, and thy soft sighs.

The Cat-Lady

Her hair is yellow as sulphur, and her gaze
As brimstone burning blue and odorous:
I know not how her eyes came to be thus
But I do think her soul must be ablaze:
Their pupils wane or wax to blame or praise;
As a cat watches mice, she watches us;
And I am sure her claws are murderous,
So feline are her velvet coaxing ways.
She purrs like a young leopard soothed and pleased
At flattery; so too turns and snarls when teased,
And pats her love like a beast of prey.
I fancy too that over wine and food
Her saffron hair turns tawny and grand her mood—
She broods like a young lioness of play.

Terrible Love

The marriage of two murderers in the gloom
Of a dark fane to hymns of blackest night;
Before a priest who keeps his hands from sight

Hidden away beneath his robe of doom,
Lest any see the flowers of blood that bloom
For gems upon the fingers, red on white;
The while far up in domes of dizzy height
The trumpets of the organ peal and boom:
Such is our love. Oh sweet delicious lips
From which I fancy all the world's blood drips!
Oh supple waist, pale cheek, and eyes of fire,
Hard little breasts and white gigantic hips,
And blue-black hair with serpent coils that slips
Out of my hand in hours of red desire.

Dedicatory Sonnet

This Haschish dream, this cup-rose heavy-leaning
    With opiums weight, this drunkenness of soul,
    Bizarre, grotesque, satiric, with strange scroll
Of flaunting fancy's wildest foliage screening
No plashy depths of philosophic meaning,
    Scoffing, believing, laughing at life's dole,
    From heart that bleeds the while to death's dear goal,
    Take, friend—my own, from no man's field a gleaning.

For I have made myself a clean new mould
    To pour my fancies in, of mad burlesque,
        Yet full of death withal as charnel air.
I first of men have carved in fancy's gold
    So queer a pagod freaked in fancy's gold,
        Though treading Wagner's ground twixt Goethe
            and Baudelaire.

ROSAMUND MARRIOTT WATSON

Walpurgis

Along the valley to the sea
　　The steel-grey river glimmers wan.
Oh, what shall this night bring to be?
　　And what may come when light be gone?

Across the dark Downs, face to face,
　　Two sullen fires flame east and west—
The blood-red sunset's lurid space,
　　The blood-red moon's uprearing crest.

A weary Mænad, flushed with wine.
　　Between the dull dun drift she peers,
Heavy with lewd old rites malign.
　　Lusting for human blood and tears.

The sea-wind holds its breath for fear.
　　The black trees cringe upon the height;
Still, with her wicked, wanton leer.
　　The red moon menaces the night.

The Golden Touch

The amber dust of sunset fills
    The limits of my narrow room,
And every sterile shadow thrills
    To golden hope, to golden bloom.

Sweet through the splendour, shrill and sweet,
    Somewhere a neighbouring cage-bird sings,
Sings of the Spring in this grey street
    While golden glories gild his wings.

Clothed with the sun he breaks to song
    In vague remembrance, deep delight
Of dim green worlds, forsaken long,
    Of leaf-hung dawn and dewy night.

My prisoning bars, transfigured too,
    Fade with the day, forsworn, forgot
Melt in a golden mist and you
    Are here, although you know it not.

AMY LEVY

Felo de Se
With Apologies to Mr. Swinburne

For repose I have sighed and have struggled; have sigh'd
    and have struggled in vain;
I am held in the Circle of Being and caught in the
    Circle of Pain.
I was wan and weary with life; my sick soul yearned for
    death;
I was weary of women and war and the sea and the wind's
    wild breath;
I cull'd sweet poppies and crush'd them, the blood ran rich
    and red:—
And I cast it in crystal chalice and drank of it till I was
    dead.
And the mould of the man was mute, pulseless in ev'ry
    part,
The long limbs lay on the sand with an eagle eating the
    heart.
Repose for the rotting head and peace for the putrid
    breast,
But for that which is "I" indeed the gods have decreed no
    rest;
No rest but an endless aching, a sorrow which grows
    amain:—

I am caught in the Circle of Being and held in the
    Circle of Pain.
Bitter indeed is Life, and bitter of Life the breath,
But give me life and its ways and its men, if this be Death.
Wearied I once of the Sun and the voices which clamour'd
    around:
Give them me back—in the sightless depths there is
    neither light nor sound.
Sick is my soul, and sad and feeble and faint as it felt
When (far, dim day) in the fair flesh-fane of the body it
    dwelt.
But then I could run to the shore, weeping and weary and
    weak;
See the waves' blue sheen and feel the breath of the breeze
    on my cheek:
Could wail with the wailing wind; strike sharply the hands
    in despair;
Could shriek with the shrieking blast, grow frenzied and
    tear the hair;
Could fight fierce fights with the foe or clutch at a human
    hand;
And weary could lie at length on the soft, sweet, saffron
    sand. . . .
I have neither a voice nor hands, nor any friend nor a foe;
I am I—just a Pulse of Pain—I am I, that is all I know.
For Life, and the sickness of Life, and Death and desire to
    die;—
They have passed away like the smoke, here is nothing but
    Pain and I.

To Vernon Lee

On Bellosguardo, when the year was young,
We wandered, seeking for the daffodil
And dark anemone, whose purples fill
The peasant's plot, between the corn-shoots sprung.

Over the grey, low wall the olive flung
Her deeper greyness; far off, hill on hill
Sloped to the sky, which, pearly-pale and still,
Above the large and luminous landscape hung.

A snowy blackthorn flowered beyond my reach;
You broke a branch and gave it to me there;
I found for you a scarlet blossom rare.

Thereby ran on of Art and Life our speech;
And of the gifts the gods had given to each—
Hope unto you, and unto me Despair.

Sinfonia Eroica

To Sylvia

My Love, my Love, it was a day in June,
A mellow, drowsy, golden afternoon;
And all the eager people thronging came
To that great hall, drawn by the magic name
Of one, a high magician, who can raise
The spirits of the past and future days,
And draw the dreams from out the secret breast,

Giving them life and shape.
                              I, with the rest,
Sat there athirst, atremble for the sound;
And as my aimless glances wandered round,
Far off, across the hush'd, expectant throng,
I saw your face that fac'd mine.
                                Clear and strong
Rush'd forth the sound, a mighty mountain stream;
Across the clust'ring heads mine eyes did seem
By subtle forces drawn, your eyes to meet.
Then you, the melody, the summer heat,
Mingled in all my blood and made it wine.
Straight I forgot the world's great woe and mine;
My spirit's murky lead grew molten fire;
Despair itself was rapture.
                              Ever higher
Stronger and clearer rose the mighty strain;
Then sudden fell; then all was still again,
And I sank back, quivering as one in pain.
Brief was the pause; then, 'mid a hush profound,
Slow on the waiting air swell'd forth a sound
So wondrous sweet that each man held his breath;
A measur'd, mystic melody of death.
Then back you lean'd your head, and I could note
The upward outline of your perfect throat;
And ever, as the music smote the air,
Mine eyes from far held fast your body fair.
And in that wondrous moment seem'd to fade
My life's great woe, and grow an empty shade
Which had not been, nor was not.
                                  And I knew
Not which was sound, and which, O Love, was you.

MAY KENDALL

Compensation

You could not love me if you knew
   The load of guilt I'm hampered by.
A life so sin-stained through and through
   Must give all love the lie.
Then hate me, for your own soul's sake,
   Or scorn, or utterly forget—
I know my heart will never break,
   While I can love you yet!

In the Drawing-Room

Furniture with the languid mien,
   On which life seems to pall—
With your insipid grey and green
   And drab, your cheerless wall—
To think that she has really been
   An hour among you all.

I wonder, since she went away,
   Has no one ever guessed
Why constantly you look more grey,
More green, and more depressed.

I know—you know, you had your day,
Now you need only rest.

Yon heavy, yellow easy-chair,
    Right opposite the door,
Ah, how impassively you stare
    Across the dreary floor;
Yet even you would be aware
    If she should come once more.

I see the dingy curtains stir
    With a faint memory;
The grand piano dreams of her
    In a drowsy minor key.
Rest tranquilly, old furniture,
    To-night it may not be!

In the Toy Shop

The child had longings all unspoken—
    She was a naughty child.
She had "a will that must be broken";
    Her brothers drove her wild.
She read the tale, but skipped the moral.
    She thought: "One *might* be good,
If one could never scream and quarrel,
    If one were only wood!"

Meanwhile the doll: "Ah, fatal chasm!
    Although I've real curls,

I am not made of protoplasm,
　　Like other little girls.
You see on every wooden feature
　　My animation's nil.
How nice to be a human creature,
　　Get cross, and have a will!"

And what may be the real issue
　　There's none hath understood;
But some of us are nervous tissue,
　　And some of us are wood.
And some to suffering, striving wildly,
　　Are never quite resigned;
While we of wood yet murmur mildly
　　At being left behind.

The Last Dance

Since whatsoe'er befall us,
　　We too have been as one,
Since the wild music calls us,
　　That now is well-nigh done—
Since I may never meet you
　　To all eternity,
Ere parting I entreat you
　　For one more dance with me.

To-night in many dances
　　We have passed mutely by,
And yet all evil chances
　　Forbade us to draw nigh.

Not thus did Fate deride me!
　　Too well my spirit knew
You only were beside me,
　　And still I danced with you!

Now the bright ranks are thinning,
　　Failing the melodies;
The pain is but beginning
　　That follows on the bliss;
Such bliss, there's no transcending
　　In realms of fadeless light—
Yet I would all were ending,
　　With our last dance to-night.

NORMAN GALE

The Sweater

Now the orchid's pinned, and he lets go slack
    In a blood-coloured car his rottening soul,
With a sealskin graveyard upon his back,
    And a corpse or two in his buttonhole.

The Mouse

In lavender-coloured silk once more
    To dare the run of luck she goes.
Right bravely on the larder floor
    The bloody dice of death she throws.

Right Royal

Sixteen gorillas butchered by a Prince
        who dared—
    A modern Cain—to lurk behind a tree!
Among the hairy half-men that he should
        have spared
    Were better men than he.

Bees

You voluble,
Velvety,
Vehement fellows
That play on your
Flying and
Musical cellos,
All goldenly
Girdled you
Senerade clover,
Each artist in
Bass but a
Bibulous rover!

You passionate,
Powdery,
Pastoral bandits,
Who gave you your
Roaming and
Rollicking mandates?
Come out of my
Foxglove; come
Out of my roses,
You bees with the
Plushy and
Plausible noses!

WILLIAM THEODORE PETERS

Cindarella Fin de Siecle

She would go to the ball.
  Her gown a pretty penny cost,
But this time it was not
  Her little slipper that she lost.

London Fog

Hopeless, fearless; in the darkness,
  With a gaze fixed, intense;
Waiting, waiting, ever waiting—
  Hell must be long suspense.

Danse des Morts
(In the Town-House of Basil)

To dance the motley measure out,
  There is the nimble task!
While scalding tears are running down
  Behind a grinning mask.

To the Café, aux Phares de l'Ouest, Quartier Montparnasse

The painted ship in the paste-board sea
    Sails night and day.
To-morrow it will be as far as it was yesterday.
    But underneath, in the *café*,
    The lusty crafts go down,
And one by one, poor mad souls drown,—
While the painted ship in the paste-board sea
    Sails night and day.

ARTHUR MACHEN

The Praise of Myfanwy

O gift of the everlasting:
O wonderful and hidden mystery.
Many secrets have been vouchsafed to me,
I have been long acquainted with the wisdom of the trees;
Ash and oak and elm have communicated to me from my
boyhood,
The birch and the hazel and all the trees of the greenwood
have not been dumb.
There is a caldron rimmed with pearls of whose gifts I am
not ignorant;
I will speak little of it; its treasures are known to the Bards.
Many went on the search of Caer-Pedryfan,
Seven alone returned with Arthur, but my spirit was present.
Seven are the apple-trees in a beautiful orchard;
I have eaten of their fruit which is not bestowed on Saxons.
I am not ignorant of a Head which is glorious and venerable;
It made perpetual entertainment for the warriors, their joys
would have been immortal;
If they had not opened the door of the south, they would
have feasted for ever,
Listening to the song of the fairy Birds of Rhiannon.
Let not anyone instruct me concerning the Glassy Isle;
In the garments of the saints who returned from it were
rich odours of Paradise.

All this I knew, and yet my knowledge was ignorance.
For one day, as I walked by Caer-rhiu in the principal
    forest of Gwent,
I saw golden Myfanwy as she bathed in the brook Tarogi,
Her hair flowed about her; Arthur's crown had dissolved
    into a shining mist.
I gazed into her blue eyes as it were into twin heavens,
All the parts of her body were adornments and miracles.
O gift of the everlasting:
O wonderful and hidden mystery:
When I embraced Myfanwy a moment became immortality.

VANCE THOMPSON

The Night Watchman

I do not think it safe to sleep,
Since He who kept the watch is dead,
And living things may prowl abroad
In the night, with none to keep
The door against them when they come.
Not safe . . . It is not safe to sleep,
Since men have killed the warder . . . God.

Ever He watched me in the night;
At two short paces from my bed
He sat, like one who keeps the guard,
His arms upon His knees, His hands
Clasped on His sword-hilt . . . eternal God,
Patient, immutable and dumb.

Now, I am here alone; the door is barred,
My window is sealed with iron bands,
Yet nightly, things that are not dead,
Enter the window and door and creep
Over the cold flags of the floor. . . .

(Ay, here even in my tower.
Knee-deep in the sands,
Girt round by the seas . . .

By the sleepless, clashing flood . . .
My tower of pride and granite stands;
And ever about it, evermore,
The sentinel winds go. . . . Over it lower
Clouds of agate and blood,
Menacing; always the clouds.)

Night comes. . . . Oh, in the night an hour,
The unavoidable hour in the night,
When every man born of woman, dreams;
And dreaming, he sees women appear,
Chained together and dragging shrouds,
(Spotted with blood like a black sky with stars)
And sleeping he groans; and his bed seems
A quadrature of molten bars;
And groaning he wakes. . . . Lo, in the darkness things
(With hands and mouths) more horrible than dreams!

O, well I know the hour
And the dream I wake from . . . here
In my violated tower . . .
Wake from . . . covered with wounds,
Dazed with the thickness of fear,
Like a black smoke} in my brain;
And a blindness in my eyes.

(I hear the familiar sounds . . .
The seas at the knees of my tower,
The gulls and their rhythmic wings
And the cries of the wind and rain.)
And here, lo, here, lo, here,
Close to my bed the living things—

Mouths like the gash of a spear,
Hands with fingers and rings,—
In the darkness the living things!

Sleep? But men have slain the Lord,
Even God, who kept the watch and ward
At two short paces from my bed,
His hands clasped on His mighty sword. . . .
Sleep? Who dare sleep now God is dead?

Daybreak

Dwarf roses and dead lavender . . .
The false, white gown of woven wool
Fain of strange lights and colorful,
Beneath the shifty lamp ablur,

A noise of tangled winds that cry
At the pale windows . . . all the high,
Uneasy winds of dawn astir,

The bruised mouth where the shadows creep,
The lips all drooping, fain of sleep,
The hot breath, heavier than myrrh;

And in the tired unholy eyes
The weariness of love that dies,
Love's faintness in the throat of her
Dwarf roses and dead lavender . . .

STUART MERRILL

The Chinese Lover's Ballade

Down the waves of the Yang-tse-Kiang,
    In a gilded barge with saffron sails,
I wooed my Li to the brazen clang
    Of kettledrums, and the weary wails
    Of flutes, whilst under her spangled veils
She would sway her willowy waist, and sing
    Sweet songs that made me dream of the dales
Of Han-Yang, Woo-hoo and far Tchin-Ting.

Past the porcelain towers of Keou-Kang,
    And its peach blooms, loud with nightingales,
We drifted fast, as the dim gongs rang,
    Toward the horizon's purple pales.
    Hark! our hoarse pilot once more hails
The anchored junks, as they swerve and swing,
    Laden with silk and balsam bales
From Han-Yang, Woo-hoo and far Tchin-Ting.

Of nights, when the hour had come to hang
    Our paper lamps to their bamboo rails,
And afar we heard the silvery twang
    Of lutes from the tea fleet's moonlit trails,
    Then, oh my Li of the jasper nails,
As on the shore swooned the winds of spring,

I lay at thy feet and told thee tales,
Of Han-Yang, Woo-hoo and far Tchin-Ting.

ENVOY

Loved Princess, ere my fantasy fails,
Farewell, and I'll make thy praises ring
O'er the Flowery Kingdom's fields and swales,
From Han-Yang, Woo-hoo to far Tchin-Ting.

Ballade of the Outcasts

THE VOICE OF THE MEN

We are the Vagabonds that sleep
In ditches by the midnight ways
Where wolves beneath the gibbets leap:
Our hands against black Fate we raise
In lifelong turmoil of affrays,
Until we die, in some dark den,
The death of dogs that hunger slays:
For we are hated of all men.

THE VOICE OF THE WOMEN

We are the Courtesans that creep
Beyond the town's lamp-litten haze,
Toward the bridges of the deep:
We watch the dawn with sinful gaze,
And dreaming of the golden days
When Jesus hallowed Magdalen,

We seek death in the river's maze:
For we are hated of all men.

THE VOICE OF THE CHILDREN

We are the Innocents that weep,
    While our bones rot with foul decays,
For all the woes that we must reap:
    No mother sings us lulling lays,
    No father o'er our slumber prays,
But forth we fare from den to den
    To filch the death-bread of the strays:
For we are hated by all men.

THE ENVOY OF THE OUTCASTS

Beware, O Kings whom Mammon sways,
Lest morrows nearer than ye ken
    With our red flags of battle blaze!
For we are hated of all men.

MARC-ANDRÉ RAFFALOVICH

Stramony

Slender and strong, and like the foxglove tall,
Rosy to match its roadside loveliness;
Like purple aconite from fierce Nepaul
Soft eyes and underlids, these coloured less;
Flesh of the peach, like peach flowers poisonous,.
Fairer than both nor scentless like the last;
And in those idle hands the black skins ooze
Of nightshade berries purple filled thou hast;
O like the hemlock dropwort in the South,
But not so kind, for through thee none forgets:
O breath benumbing, O narcotic mouth!
Faint anodyne like scented violets;
    And like the foxglove, chill at first to me,
    But wilder tasted than red stramony.

On the Borderland of Sin

Here in these love-surrounded solitudes
I make of sleep a place to watch you in,
While silence through close carven branches thin
With moonlit footsteps creeps in fancied woods;
And stealthy pink thorn over us excludes
The sky from nearer kissing of your skin,

From any breezes vocal with faint sin
My lordship of your cold unconscious moods.

Unseen, untouched, beneath a dreamt-of bliss,
I dare not stir the blossom of a kiss:
For at the first disturbing of the air
Would not the pink thorn petals, round and sweet,
Like many flakes of blood on limbs and hair,
Flutter and quiver to your weary feet?

Blue and Orange

Blue sky, blue sea, blue butterflies,
An orange grove, and your blue eyes;
How young the world was, and we two,
Proud Robbers of the Golden Fleece,
Young Jason I, Medea you! . . .
Blue tights and blue electric glare,
Blue cornflowers in your orange hair,
A tight-rope dancer's fixed eyes, blue,
An orange sash, an orange fan,
A music-hall magician you!

Love, Vice, Crime, and Sin

The lips of Vice were painted,
    The face of Vice was white,
Love passed on unacquainted,
    Intent on Love's delight.

And though Love's heart beat faster
　　Beneath the eyes of Crime,
His breath he strove to master,
　　And hummed a foolish rhyme.

But when the sun was shining
　　Love reached a shadowy place,
And there at last reclining
　　Sin had his true love's face.

The Green Carnation

The flowers of love are not expensive flowers,
And children idly pluck them as they pass,
And happy lovers in their happiest hours,
Walking together on the flower-soft grass:
Sweet violets, when violets are due,
Pinks, daisies, privet, lilac, sorrel, clover,
Weeds, wayside flowers, and flowers from gardens, too!
And when love tires, and love for love is over,
Love's other moods in other flowers delight,
Voluptuous, tawdry, evil, tuberoses,
Orchids uncouth, foxglove or aconite—
But never in his chaste or poisonous posies
Can love allow this milliner's creation,
This shilling shocker, once a white carnation.

LAURENCE HOPE

Malaria

He lurks among the reeds, beside the marsh,
 Red oleanders twisted in His hair,
His eyes are haggard and His lips are harsh,
 Upon His breast the bones show gaunt and bare.

The green and stagnant waters lick his feet,
 And from their filmy, iridescent scum
Clouds of mosquitoes, gauzy in the heat,
 Rise with His gifts: Death and Delirium.

His messengers: they bear the deadly taint
 On spangled wings aloft and far away,
Making thin music, strident and yet faint,
 From golden eve to silver break of day.

The baffled sleeper hears th' incessant whine
 Through his tormented dreams, and finds no rest.
The thirsty insects use his blood for wine,
 Probe his blue veins and pasture on his breast.

While far away He in the marshes lies,
 Staining the stagnant water with His breath,
An endless hunger burning in His eyes,
 A famine unassuaged, whose food is Death.

He hides among the ghostly mists that float
   Over the water, weird and white and chill,
And peasants, passing in their laden boat,
   Shiver and feel a sense of coming ill.

A thousand burn and die; He takes no heed,
   Their bones, unburied, strewn upon the plain,
Only increase the frenzy of His greed
   To add more victims to th' already slain.

He loves the haggard frame, the shattered mind,
   Gloats with delight upon the glazing eye,
Yet, in one thing His cruelty is kind,
   He sends them lovely dreams before they die;

Dreams that bestow on them their heart's desire,
   Visions that find them mad, and leave them blest,
To sink, forgetful of the fever's fire,
   Softly, as in a lover's arms, to rest.

"To the Unattainable"

Oh, that my blood were water, thou athirst,
And thou and I in some far Desert land,
How would I shed it gladly, if but first
It touched thy lips, before it reached the sand.

Once,—ah, the Gods were good to me,—I threw
Myself upon a poison snake, that crept

Where my Beloved—a lesser love we knew
Than this which now consumes me wholly—slept.

But thou; alas, what can I do for thee?
By Fate, and thine own beauty, set above
The need of all or any aid from me,
Too high for service, as too far for love.

Opium:
Li's Riverside Hut at Taku

The room is bare, the paper windows shiver,
    Beneath the ill-hung door, the sleet blows free,
Yet here. Delight flows forth, a gentle river,
    To saturate my soul with ecstasy!

I lie upon the heated *Kang,* quiescent,
    Lulled by the warmth of lighted straw below,
While Li, the golden-tinted adolescent,
    Blue-clad and silent, passes to and fro.

Li, with his well-cut lips and supple fingers,
    His crudely lidded eyes, that seem to gaze
Back through ten thousand years of thought, where lingers
    Some misty splendour of the old, old days.

Free from the plait, his loosened sable tresses
    In silken waves, below the knee, descend.
Bringing the opium pipe, he deftly presses
    The viscous drug upon the needle's end.

Lights it, inserts it in the pipe beside me,
    Then through my lips the magic vapour streams,
And Life and Love, that seldom satisfied me,
    Meet me with lovely faces in my dreams.

Life at his brightest, flushed and crowned with flowers,
    Brings gifts no mortal, waking, e'er possessed.
Exquisite Chances, and Enchanted Hours,
    While Love,—Love brings me you, to share my rest!

CHARLES SAYLE

Poenitentia

The brazen trumpets clang and bray
Above God's golden House to-day,
The saffron-scented torches flare
High up upon the dancing air,
And everywhere new echoes fall
Most rapturously musical:—
It seems as though High Heaven were bent
Upon some new-wrought Sacrament.

With lute and lyre they hie along,
With flute and pipe the angel throng;
While here the sound of violins,
Responding to their call begins,
And dulcimers so lightly played
Join in the chorus that is made.—
O what hath chanced in Dome and Hall
To bring them thus to festival?

Gaudium est in coelo, hear
Strains immortal strike the ear,
Super uno peccatore
Pumitentiam agente.
Gaudium! the chorus sings
Loud above the cithern strings,
And high above the petulant drum
Angels answer, *Gaudium!*

ARTHUR SYMONS

Bianca

Her cheeks are hot, her cheeks are white;
The white girl hardly breathes to-night,
   So faint the pulses come and go,
   That waken to a smouldering glow
The morbid faintness of her white.

What drowsing heats of sense, desire
Longing and languorous, the fire
   Of what white ashes, subtly mesh
   The fascination of her flesh
Into a breathing web of fire?

Only her eyes, only her mouth,
Live, in the agony of drouth,
   Athirst for that which may not be:
   The desert of virginity
Aches in the hotness of her mouth.

I take her hands into my hands,
Silently, and she understands;
   I set my lips upon her lips;
   Shuddering to her finger-tips
She strains my hands within her hands.

I set my lips on hers; they close
Into a false and phantom rose;
    Upon her thirsting lips I rain
    A flood of kisses, and in vain;
Her lips inexorably close.

Through her closed lips that cling to mine,
Her hands that hold me and entwine,
    Her body that abondoned lies,
    Rigid with sterile ecstasies,
A shiver knits her flesh to mine.

Life sucks into a mist remote
Her fainting lips, her throbbing throat;
    Her lips that open to my lips,
    And, hot against her finger-tips,
The pulses leaping in her throat.

The Absinthe Drinker

Gently I wave the visible world away.
    Far off, I hear a roar, afar yet near,
    Far off and strange, a voice is in my ear,
And is the voice my own? the words I say
Fall strangely, like a dream, across the day;
    And the dim sunshine is a dream. How clear,
    New as the world to lovers' eyes, appear
The men and women passing on their way!
The world is very fair. The hours are all
    Linked in a dance of mere forgetfulness.
      I am at peace with God and man. O glide,

Sands of the hour-glass that I count not, fall
   Serenely: scarce I feel your soft caress.
      Rocked on this dreamy and indifferent tide.

Morbidezza

White girl, your flesh is lilies
Grown 'neath a frozen moon,
So still is
The rapture of your swoon
Of whiteness, snow or lilies.
The virginal revealment,
Your bosom's wavering slope,
Concealment,
'Neath fainting heliotrope,
Of whitest white's revealment,
Is like a bed of lilies,
A jealous-guarded row,
Whose will is
Simply chaste dreams:—but oh,
The alluring scent of lilies!

DOUGLAS AINSLIE

The Death of Verlaine

> "Rien de plus cher que la chanson grise."
> —Verlaine

So the poet of grey slips away,
    The poor singer from over the strait,
Who sat by the Paris highway,
    Whose life was the laughter of fate;

The laughter of fate, but the woe
    Of the gods and the mortals who heard
The mystical modes as they flow—
    Broken phrase, riven lute, broken word,

Broken up as the attar is crushed
    By the steel of the mercantile weights
From the soul of the roses that blushed
    Through the scroll of Elysian gates.

As a sphynx-moth with shivering wings
    Hangs over the thyme in the garden
But an instant, then fairyward brings
    The honey he gathers for guerdon;

So you the oases of life
    Just touched with your frayed, rapid wings,
Poor poet, and drew from the strife
    The peculiar honey that clings

To your magical measures and ways,
    As they sway with the moods of the soul,
Semi-conscious, through haze, in amaze,
    Making on toward a dim distant goal.

"Be always a poet or saint"—
    Poor Lélian was saint and was poet,
But not always for sometimes we faint—
    Then he must forget that we know it;

In iris and opal forget—
    His iris, his bow in the sky,
Fickle bow for the storm, and that yet
    Was his only storm-bow to steer by.

Good-bye, then, poor poet, good-bye!
    You will not be long there alone:
Very soon for your help we shall cry,
    Lost souls in a country unknown.

Then Lélian, king of the land,
    Rich Lélian will teach us the speech
That here we but half understand—
    Kind Lélian will reach us his hand.

Her Colours

Rose, grey, and white—
Roses, sad seas, and light
Straight from the sun—
 These are your colours.

Red necklet spun
When the Eastern day was done
By fairy fingers
 Of lotus flowers.

In those white ivories
Your arms, a charm there lies,
Charm to conquer
 The bravest singers:

And for your grey
Sweet, deep eye oceans—they
 Do yet declare
 Queen Venus lingers.

The Vampire and the Dove

I dreamed I saw a Vampire seize a Dove,
Chief Chariot-bearer of the Car of Love.
Her feathers ivory white did strew the ground,
Her neck that with her glossy head was crowned
Shewed a red wound where Vampire's lips were pressed,
Languid it drooped upon her panting breast.
I dreamed I woke, I dreamed the dream was true,

I dreamed, beloved, that the Dove was you.
I dreamed I dreamed again, and, lo! the brand
Of Perseus sudden came into my hand;
I dreamed I plunged it in the Vampire's side
Up to the hilt; I dreamed the Vampire died,
With horrid quivering of its leathery wings,
With claws all bloodèd and with mouth that stings,
Fallen from my Dove; I dreamed a woman's face
Glared upward on me from the Vampire's place.
But for the Dove her gentle head upraised
Resumed perfection, cooingly she praised
This deed of mine, with wounded neck come whole,
While from her eyes shone forth on mine your soul.
No more I dreamed, but woke and waking knew,
O my beloved, that the dream was true.

ROBINSON KAY LEATHER

Bubbles

'Tis sweet at noontide from the glare
And hot thick traffic otherwhere
To pause where hangs some picture rare
  Of meadow grass unmown;
And sweeter 'tis 'mid thicker strife
That grows about our growing life
To meet a boy whose years are brief
  And all the world unknown.

While at our pipe we puff amain—
A sweet narcotic from the brain
To keep aloof its thoughts of pain—
  See him with joyous care,
That grows from nothing into sight,
A bubble, rainbow-hued and light
As his boy's fancy, with delight
  Let float into the air.

And as the bubble through the room,
Of its frail beauty venturesome,
Nowhither bound from nowhere come,
  Passes with passing show,
In idle mood we moralize,
"'Tis better to be fool than wise,
To run the race than hold the prize,
  And not to know than know."

RICHARD LE GALLIENNE

The Décadent to His Soul

The Décadent was speaking to his soul—
Poor useless thing, he said,
Why did God burden me with such as thou?
The body were enough,
The body gives me all.

The soul's a sort of sentimental wife
That prays and whimpers of the higher life,
Objects to latch-keys, and bewails the old,
The dear old days, of passion and of dream,
When life was a blank canvas, yet untouched
Of the great painter Sin.

Yet, little soul, thou hast fine eyes,
And knowest fine airy motions,
Hast a voice—
Why wilt thou so devote them to the church?

His face grew strangely sweet—
As when a toad smiles.
He dreamed of a new sin:
An incest 'twixt the body and the soul.

He drugged his soul, and in a house of sin
She played all she remembered out of heaven

For him to kiss and clip by.
He took a little harlot in his hands,
And she made all his veins like boiling oil,
Then that grave organ made them cool again.

Then from that day, he used his soul
As bitters to the over dulcet sins,
As olives to the fatness of the feast—
She made those dear heart-breaking ecstasies
Of minor chords amid the Phrygian flutes,
She sauced his sins with splendid memories,
Starry regrets and infinite hopes and fears;
His holy youth and his first love
Made pearly background to strange-coloured vice.

Sin is no sin when virtue is forgot.
It is so good in sin to keep in sight
The white hills whence we fell, to measure by—
To say I was so high, so white, so pure,
And am so low, so blood-stained and so base;
I revel here amid the sweet sweet mire
And yonder are the hills of morning flowers;
So high, so low; so lost and with me yet;
To stretch the octave 'twixt the dream and deed,
Ah, that's the thrill!
To dream so well, to do so ill,—
There comes the bitter-sweet that makes the sin.

First drink the stars, then grunt amid the mire,
So shall the mire have something of the stars,
And the high stars be fragrant of the mire.

The Décadent was speaking to his soul—
Dear witch, I said the body was enough.
How young, how simple as a suckling child!
And then I dreamed—"an incest 'twixt the body and the
    soul:"
Let's wed, I thought, the seraph with the dog,
And wait the purple thing that shall be born.

And now look round-seest thou this bloom?
Seven petals and each petal seven dyes,
The stem is gilded and the root in blood:
That came of thee.
Yea, all my flowers were single save for thee.
I pluck seven fruits from off a single tree,
I pluck seven flowers from off a single stem,
I light my palace with the seven stars,
And eat strange dishes to Gregorian chants:
All thanks to thee.

But the soul wept with hollow hectic face,
Captive in that lupanar of a man.
And I who passed by heard and wept for both,—
The man was once an apple-cheek dear lad,
The soul was once an angel up in heaven.

O let the body be a healthy beast,
And keep the soul a singing soaring bird;
But lure thou not the soul from out the sky
To pipe unto the body in the sty.

JOHN GRAY

Complaint

To Felix Fénéon

Men, women, call thee so or so;
   I do not know.
   Thou hast no name
For me, but in my heart aflame

Burns tireless, neath a silver vine.
   And round entwine
   Its purple girth
All things of fragrance and of worth.

Thou shout! thou burst of light! thou throb
   Of pain! thou sob!
   Thou like a bar
Of some sonata, heard from far

Through blue-hue'd veils! When in these wise,
   To my soul's eyes,
   Thy shape appears,
My aching hands are full of tears.

Summer Past

To Oscar Wilde

There was the summer. There
   Warm hours of leaf-lipped song,
   And dripping amber sweat.
     O sweet to see
The great trees condescend to cast a pearl
Down to the myrtles; and the proud leaves curl
     In ecstasy.

Fruit of a quest, despair.
Smart of a sullen wrong.
Where may they hide them yet?
     One hour, yet one,
To find the mossgod lurking in his nest,
To see the naiads' floating hair, caressed
     By fragrant sun-

   Beams. Softly lulled the eves
   The song-tired birds to sleep,
   That other things might tell
     Their secrecies.
The beetle humming neath the fallen leaves.
Deep in what hollow do the stern gods keep
Their bitter silence? By what listening well
     Where holy trees,

Song-set, unfurl eternally the sheen
     Of restless green?

Poem

To Arthur Edmonds

Geranium, houseleek, laid in oblong beds
On the trim grass. The daisies' leprous stain
Is fresh. Each night the daisies burst again,
Though every day the gardener crops their heads.

A wistful child, in foul unwholesome shreds,
Recalls some legend of a daisy chain
That makes a pretty necklace. She would fain
Make one, and wear it, if she had some threads.

Sun, leprous flowers, foul child. The asphalt burns.
The garrulous sparrows perch on metal Burns.
Sing! Sing! they say, and flutter with their wings.
He does not sing, he only wonders why
He is sitting there. The sparrows sing. And I
Yield to the strait allure of simple things.

DORA SIGERSON SHORTER

Beware

I closed my hands upon a moth
    And when I drew my palms apart,
Instead of dusty, broken wings
    I found a bleeding human heart.

I crushed my foot upon a worm
    That had my garden for its goal,
But when I drew my foot aside
    I found a dying human soul.

ALTHEA GYLES

Sympathy

The colour gladdens all your heart;
You call it Heaven, dear, but I—
Now Hope and I are far apart—
Call it the sky.

I know that Nature's tears have wet
The world with sympathy; but you—
Who know not any sorrow yet—
Call it the dew.

From Rosamor Dead to Favonius for whom She Died

You loved my rounded cheeks!
They have grown thin and white,
You loved my carmine lips!
They give no more delight.

You loved my flame bright hair!
Quenched now its gleaming gold.
You loved my fragrant flesh!
'Tis waxen stark and cold.

But ah! the one thing, Dear,
You did not love in me,
Blooms soft, and red, and gold,
Fragrant immortally.

Not you, nor Time, nor Death,
Have any power to move
One crimson petal from
My perfect rose of Love.

Yet when death calls to you
The breath of Love shall part
The petals of my Rose
And bare its burning heart.

GASCOIGNE MACKIE

At Clapham Junction
(Nov. 13th, 1895)

Ah—as the Cretan stag might trail
The hunter's cruel arrow—
Αἴλινον εἴπέ—echo wail—
They pierce my bones and marrow.

The hounds are loose upon my track,
The rabble hoot and hollo!
Have they not branded on my back
Thine arrows, Oh Apollo?

Yet perfect none the less will peer
The flowers in Magdalen meadow,
And every daffodil next year
Will cast an oval shadow.

The crocus, gold and gray, will flame;
The blond and streak'd fritillary:—
Though I stand bowed with bitter shame
And handcuff'd in the pillory.

I shall survive the mob's malign
Mean "digito monstrari":
One must be damned to be divine—
Hurl me to hell—what care I?

Though Time's dark banks, as Time runs by
To-morrow and to-morrow,
Re-echo "Oscar" to the cry
Of outraged love and sorrow—

Out of the ashes of my lust
A Phoenix re-arisen
I shall emerge, spurning the dust
And infamy of prison.

The poets will be on my side
And they shall tell my story—
The legend of my sin and pride
Shall last till Time be hoary.

LIONEL JOHNSON

Vinum Daemonum

To Stephen Phillips

The crystal flame, the ruby flame,
Alluring, dancing, revelling!
See them: and ask me not, whence came
    This cup I bring.

But only watch the wild wine glow,
But only taste its fragrance: then,
Drink the wild drink I bring, and so
    Reign among men.

Only one sting, and then but joy:
One pang of fire, and thou art free.
Then, what thou wilt, thou canst destroy:
    Save only me!

Triumph in tumult of thy lust:
Wanton in passion of thy will:
Cry *Peace!* to conscience, and it must
    At last be still.

I am the Prince of this World: I
Command the flames, command the fires.

Mine are the draughts, that satisfy
   This World's desires.

Thy longing leans across the brink:
Ah, the brave thirst within thine eyes!
For there is that within this drink,
   Which never dies.

The Age of a Dream

To Christopher Whall

Imageries of dreams reveal a gracious age:
Black armour, falling lace, and altar lights at morn.
The courtesy of saints, their gentleness and scorn,
Lights on an earth more fair, than shone from Plato's page:
The courtesy of knights, fair calm and sacred rage:
The courtesy of love, sorrow for love's sake borne.
Vanished, those high conceits! Desolate and forlorn,
We hunger against hope for the lost heritage.

Gone now, the cavern work! Ruined, the golden shrine!
No more the glorious organs pour their voice divine;
No more the frankincense drifts through the Holy Place:
Now from the broken tower, what solemn bell still tolls,
Mourning what piteous death? Answer, O saddened souls!
Who mourn the death of beauty and the death of grace.

LOUIS BARSAC

A Grey Morning

A dull-eyed morning, only half awake;
Black pyramids of lace against the grey—
Through naked boughs the trees let in the day;
The mist-fringed hills a faint blue blurring make
Where on the shore of sky earth-billows break;
The sleepy river winds its sinuous way
Where shrivell'd reeds ungainly limbs display,
And long lank stems lean down their lips to slake;
The hulking breeze slinks past without a sound,
Save where it frays against the straggled leaves
That still upon some shelter'd branch are found,
Or with a low, half-stifled growl upheaves
The clustering heaps upon the sodden'd ground,
And round my heart a shroud of sadness weaves.

The Poppies

Dreaming Willie sat one morning
    In the corn,
Buried in a wealth of poppies,
    Blood-red poppies,
Wondering how their bloom was born.

"Say," he whisper'd to the poppies,
    "If you can,
How you won that wealth of colour,
    Blazing colour,
Were you not once white and wan?"

Bending low, the modest poppies,
    Whispering, said,
"We can read the thoughts of mortals,
    Sin-woo'd mortals,
And 'tis blushing makes us red."

Did He Know?

Did He know when He made the world
    ("He of the lightning eyes")
How seas of tears and tides of blood,
A drear unfathomable flood,
Should soon engulf the scented meads
In noisome slime and fetid weeds,
        Did He know?
    Or is it all a great surprise?

Without Form and Void

I love the things that crouch with dusky faces,
    Blunt-edged against the brooding day,
The things that fill no finely-sculptured spaces,
    But shrink unoutlined in the grey.

The formless clouds that flap around the moon,
  The tumbling vapours on the fells,
The wandering notes that never shape a tune,
  The half-dream'd tale that no one tells.

Those misty things held loose in shadowy hands,
  That hesitate to do or be,
Which hasty man nor speaks nor understands,
  Dim inklings of Infinity.

Vision

Hosts march and shine on high,
  But his slow sight is dim;
The war lords of the sky
  Lift no bright hoof for him

Till blinding mists arise,
  And then the hidden stars
Troop straight into his eyes,
  White gods on silver cars.

SANDYS WASON

Kabale und Liebe

Many a mad magenta minute
Lights the lavender of life;
Keran-Happuch at her spinet
Psalms the scarlet song of strife:
Keran-Happuch is my wife.

Spinet carving olive stanzas,
Orange fricassees of sound,
Nicotine extravaganzas,
Like a cheese at evening found,
Sitting primrose on the ground!

Spinet, squirt thy chiaroscuro
On the omelette of the past,
Bathe our elegiac bureau,
Bind thy nightshirt to the mast—
Chocolate with the lenten fast!

Never sing thy mauve November
O'er the treacle crest of Hope,
With a harsh, peagreen "Remember"
Baked in a kaleidoscope:
Buttercup—then Heliotrope.

Never—but my satin hookah
Swims to meet spring's blue decay.
Whispering to each green onlooker,
like a curried castaway,
"Ah! the midnight of the Day!"

ERNEST DOWSON

Non Sum Qualis Eram Bonae Sub Regno Cynarae

Last night, ah, yesternight, betwixt her lips and mine
There fell thy shadow, Cynara! thy breath was shed
Upon my soul between the kisses and the wine;
And I was desolate and sick of an old passion,
    Yea, I was desolate and bowed my head:
I have been faithful to thee, Cynara! in my fashion.

All night upon mine heart I felt her warm heart beat,
Night-long within mine arms in love and sleep she lay;
Surely the kisses of her bought red mouth were sweet;
But I was desolate and sick of an old passion,
    When I awoke and found the dawn was gray:
I have been faithful to thee, Cynara! in my fashion.

I have forgot much, Cynara! gone with the wind,
Flung roses, roses riotously with the throng,
Dancing, to put thy pale, lost lilies out of mind;
But I was desolate and sick of an old passion,
    Yea, all the time, because the dance was long:
I have been faithful to thee, Cynara! in my fashion.

I cried for madder music and for stronger wine,
But when the feast is finished and the lamps expire,

Then falls thy shadow, Cynara! the night is thine;
And I am desolate and sick of an old passion,
    Yea, hungry for the lips of my desire:
I have been faithful to thee, Cynara! in my fashion

Dregs

The fire is out, and spent the warmth thereof
(This is the end of every song man sings!)
The golden wine is drunk, the dregs remain,
Bitter as wormwood and as salt as pain;
And health and hope have gone the way of love
Into the drear oblivion of lost things.
Ghosts go along with us until the end;
This was a mistress, this, perhaps, a friend.
With pale, indifferent eyes, we sit and wait
For the dropt curtain and the closing gate:
This is the end of all the songs man sings.

GEORGE IVES

I Can Trust Thee

I can trust thee throughout the common day,
Close by my side or absent far away,
Meet with a quiet smile
Those who would thee revile
And so betray.

I can trust thee where sleep's wide wings extend,
When only closing lids my soul defend
From chance or charm,
And ghostly harm.
Or evil trend.

I can trust thee when fever's fiery blast
Tears through the blood, and, reason overcast.
Earth sinks away.
Night follows day,
And dreams whirl past.

I could trust thee to guide my lonely soul
Through gulfs of space where great stars roll
To Heaven's bright door,
Where we once more
Shall be one whole.

Young God of Love

Young God of Love,
Crowned with quadruple
Elemental stars,
The diamonds
Of thy circling coronal.

And then five rubies
Flashing jacinth light
Of passion from thy brow.
One for each sense,
Blushed against their white purity.

To Slander

Vain to pour
Corrosive drops of spite
Into the golden chalice of my love.
Copper acquaintance
And tin courtesy
Might melt and smoke
Before that acrid stream;
But love's bright gold
Receives it as the harmless
Meadow dew,
And shines undimmed.

PARIS, 1898.

SADAKICHI HARTMANN

As the Lindens Shiver in Autumn Dreams

The fields lie wrapt in autumn dreams,
   Beneath the din, blue vault of night,
      The moon, like a bark on sluggish streams,
         Spreads soft her sail of silver light.

Beneath the blue, dim vault of night,
   With the way-worn notes of joy and care,
      Across the sea of the moon's pale light
         Dark flocks of birds flap the silent air.

With the way-worn notes of joy and care
   Fantastic shapes with wings outspread,
      Dark flocks of birds flap the silent air,
         Like a cloud of ominous dread.

Fantastic shapes with wings outspread,
   Droning some harsh and ghoulish tune,
      Like a cloud of ominous dread,
         They darken the sail of the white full moon.

They darken the sail of the soft white moon,
   Like pageants of some Valpurgis night,
      Droning some harsh and ghoulish tune,
         Their rustling wings are shimmering bright.

Their rustling wings are shimmering bright
As in myriad swarms they are passing by,
Like pageants of some Valpurgis night,
Wheeling their flight to some summer sky.

Wheeling their flight whence summer has flown,
Like dreams and hopes now long gone by,
Like songs of love our youth has known,
In myriad swarms they sail the sky.

Like clouds a-sail on glassy streams—
Grey memories of autumn dreams;—
Like visions of love forever flown,
You, aerial voyagers, wing your flight
To some enchanted realm our youth has known,
Beneath the dim, blue vault of night.

VINCENT O'SULLIVAN

Malaria

At sunset, when the shifting light
    Fails in the marshes, what most fair
And sombre Spirit, robed in night,
    Comes floating down the waves of air?

Hot air that takes away control
    From all my body's nerves, and falls
Like scented water through my soul.
    Miasmas spread like perfumed palls.

A violet and yellow flush
    Floats to intense skies like a spire:
It bathes my heart with secret hush
    And fills my brain with dreaming fire.

Poison, dark goddess, is thy name!
    Beside the rank and stagnant pool
Where thou dost live, there is no shame
    In thy embrace: thy bed is cool.

Come, ere appears the steadfast line
    Of outpost stars ah! let thy breath
Kiss me, and press thy breast to mine,
    Thou sweet grave harbinger of Death.

Drug

When winds scream round the corners damp and chilly,
And clouds of rain blot out the gas-lamp's flare,
While lean-faced, pale-eyed men take stand and glare
Upon the sin-soiled floor of Piccadilly,
And harlots of the pavement fling their silly
Maniac laughter in their great despair
Sweet Drug! 'tis thou who draw'st me thence, to where
Sways languidly the dew-embroidered lily.

Light up the dusky caverns of my soul,
Light up the dead oppressive days, and shine,
Miraculous life-giver! where the scroll
Of hours is spent and charred: ah, come and twine
Thy soft arms round me! Now let tempests roll;
The pageant of thy spirit blends with mine.

Shadows

The passionate flowers with their wild surrender
Of colours and sweets they garbed at dawn,
The tumbling bees, and oh, the tender
Shadows of birds all over the lawn.

Often at night I see fair old places
Where linger the ghosts I would fain forget
Ah, they sleep a sleep, those white dead faces
Too sound for dreaming as I dream yet.

GEORGE STERLING

A Mood

I am grown weary of permitted things
    And weary of the care-emburdened age—
    Of any dusty lore of priest and sage
To which no memory of Arcadia clings;
For subtly in my blood at evening sings
    A madness of the faun—a choric rage
    That makes all earth and sky seem but a cage
In which the spirit pines with cheated wings.

Rather by dusk for Lilith would I wait
    And for a moment's rapture welcome death,
Knowing that I had baffled Time and Fate,
      And feeling on my lips, that died with day
    As sense and soul were gathered to a breath,
      The immortal, deadly lips that kissing slay.

PERCY OSBORN

Heartsease and Orchid

Heartsease it was from his dear hand I took,
A dainty flower that loves the garden air,
Breathing the freshness of his boyhood fair.
So it was treasured in a garden brook.

There came another with a far off look,
His hand an orchid gave; 'twas strange and rare,
And caught my senses in a beauteous snare,
Till sunlight for the furnace I forsook.

My heart grew drowsy with a sweet disease;
And fluttered in a cage of fantasy;
And I remembered how his face was pale,
Yet by its very paleness more did please;
Now hath the orchid grown a part of me,
But still the heartsease tells its olden tale.

LORD ALFRED DOUGLAS

Two Loves

To "The Spinx"

Two loves I have of comfort and despair
The like two spirits do suggest me still,
My better angel is a man right fair,
My worse a woman tempting me to ill.
—*Shakespeare.*

I dreamed I stood upon a little hill,
And at my feet there lay a ground, that seemed
Like a waste garden, flowering at its will
With buds and blossoms. There were pools that dreamed
Black and unruffled; there were white lilies
A few, and crocuses, and violets
Purple or pale, snake-like fritillaries
Scarce seen for the rank grass, and through green nets
Blue eyes of shy pervenche winked in the sun.
And there were curious flowers, before unknown,
Flowers that were stained with moonlight, or with shades
Of Nature's wilful moods; and here a one
That had drunk in the transitory tone
Of one brief moment in a sunset; blades
Of grass that in an hundred springs had been

Slowly but exquisitely nurtured by the stars,
And watered with the scented dew long cupped
In lilies, that for rays of sun had seen
Only God's glory, for never a sunrise mars
The luminous air of Heaven. Beyond, abrupt,
A grey stone wall, o'erarown with velvet moss
Uprose; and gazing I stood long, all mazed
To see a place so strange, so sweet, so fair.
And as I stood and marvelled, lo! across
The garden came a youth; one hand he raised
To shield him from the sun, his wind-tossed hair
Was twined with flowers, and in his hand he bore
A purple bunch of bursting grapes, his eyes
Were clear as crystal, naked all was he,
White as the snow on pathless mountains frore,
Red were his lips as red wine-spilth that dyes
A marble floor, his brow chalcedony.
And he came near me, with his lips uncurled
And kind, and caught my hand and kissed my mouth,
And gave me grapes to eat, and said, "Sweet friend,
Come, I will show thee shadows of the world
And images of life. See from the South
Comes the pale pageant that hath never an end."
And lo! within the garden of my dream
I saw two walking on a shining plain
Of golden light. The one did joyous seem
And fair and blooming, and a sweet refrain
Came from his lips; he sang of pretty maids
And joyous love of comely girl and boy,
His eyes were bright, and 'mid the dancing blades
Of golden grass his feet did trip for joy;

And in his hand he held an ivory lute
With strings of gold that were as maidens' hair,
And sang with voice as tuneful as a flute,
And round his neck three chains of roses were.
But he that was his comrade walked aside;
He was full sad and sweet, and his large eyes
Were strange with wondrous brightness, staring wide
With gazing; and he sighed with many sighs
That moved me, and his cheeks were wan and white
Like pallid lilies, and his lips were red
Like poppies, and his hands he clenched tight,
And yet again unclenched, and his head
Was wreathed with moon-flowers pale as lips of death.
A purple robe he wore, o'erwrought in gold
With the device of a great snake, whose breath
Was fiery flame: which when I did behold
I fell a-weeping, and I cried, "Sweet youth,
Tell me why, sad and sighing, thou dost rove
These pleasent realms? I pray thee speak me sooth
What is thy name?" He said, "My name is Love."
Then straight the first did turn himself to me
And cried, "He lieth, for his name is Shame,
But I am Love, and I was wont to be
Alone in this fair garden, till he came
Unasked by night; I am true Love, I fill
The hearts of boy and girl with mutual flame."
Then sighing, said the other, "Have thy will,
I am the love that dare not speak its name."

In Praise of Shame

Last night unto my bed methought there came
Our lady of strange dreams, and from an urn
She poured live fire, so that mine eyes did burn
At sight of it. Anon the floating flame
Took many shapes, and one cried: I am Shame
That walks with Love, I am most wise to turn
Cold lips and limbs to fire; therefore discern
And see my loveliness, and praise my name.

And afterwards, in radiant garments dressed
With sound of flutes and laughing of glad lips,
A pomp of all the passions passed along
All the night through; till the white phantom ships
Of dawn sailed in. Whereat I said this song,
"Of all sweet passions Shame is loveliest."

Impressions de Nuit
London

See what a mass of gems the city wears
Upon her broad live bosom! row on row
Rubies and emeralds and amethysts glow.
See! that huge circle like a necklace, stares
With thousands of bold eyes to heaven, and dares
The golden stars to dim the lamps below,
And in the mirror of the mire I know
The moon has left her image unawares.

That's the great town at night: I see her breasts,
Pricked out with lamps they stand like huge black towers.
I think they move! I hear her panting breath.
And that's her head where the tiara rests.
And in her brain, through lanes as dark as death,
Men creep like thoughts . . . The lamps are like pale flowers.

The Sphinx

I gaze across the Nile; flamelike and red
The sun goes down, and all the western sky
Is drowned in sombre crimson; wearily
A great bird flaps along with wings of lead,
Black on the rose-red river. Over my head
The sky is hard green bronze, beneath me lie
The sleeping ships; there is no sound, or sigh
Of the wind's breath, a stillness of the dead.

Over a palm tree's top I see the peaks
Of the tall pyramids; and though my eyes
Are barred from it, I know that on the sand
Crouches a thing of stone that in some wise
Broods on my heart; and from the darkening land
Creeps Fear and to my soul in whisper speaks.

LADY ALIX EGERTON

Phantoms

A horror of great darkness hangs round me,
The air is thick and black and filled with forms,
Which loom and change and pass and loom again;
Flat, viscous, shapeless faces, white, obscene,
With eyes that squint and scowl, and some that gaze
Medusa-like, and almost freeze my blood;
With lips betokening every sin in hell,
That writhe and leer and mouth some awful word.
These forms, I see, have hands, long skinny hands,
Some are like claws, crooked and bent with greed,
And there are damp thick fleshy hands that ooze,
While one or two are dripped and stained with blood.
So, in the fearful silence of the dark,
I feel their soundless moving round my bed,
I see the hands stretch out to clutch at me,
While I lie cowering, voiceless, vision-bound,
Knowing if one should touch me I should die.

CHRISTOPHER JOHN BRENNAN

Nox Marmorea

This night is not of gentle draperies
or cluster'd banners where the star-breaths roam,
nor hangs above the torch a lurching dome
of purple gloom that slips with phantom ease;

but, on our listlessness encroaching, these,
stable, whose smooth defiance none hath clomb,
basalt and jade, a patience of the gnome,
polish'd and shadow-brimm'd transparencies.

Far, where our oubliette is closed, above,
we guess the ample lids that never move
beneath her brows, that massive arch inert

hung high-contemptuous o'er the blatant wars
we deem'd well-waged for her who may avert
some Janus-face that smiles on hidden stars.

THEODORE WRATISLAW

After Death

Though desert sands or ruined stones
Lie heavy upon my buried head,
Though worms within my skull are fed
Or jackals on my putrid bones,

Though the sea ever-chafing moans
Above my limbs long-washed and dead,
Doubt not my spirit will be led
By thy sweet voice's tender tones.

Fear not, if, when you vainly weep
At midnight for reluctant sleep,
You feel an unseen presence bow

Toward you, and through the shuddering air
Press down cold hands amid your hair
And chilly kisses on your brow.

In the Ball-room

Here where the swaying dancers float,
The heady perfume swimming round
Your slender arms and virginal throat
Thrills me though riper loves abound.

The passionate eyes and lids of her
Whose face gleams white in many a fold
Of coiling wondrous sombre hair,
The blue eyes in the wreath of gold,

These turn to me in vain, who prize
You more than all the loves and lyres,
For from your unfilled corsage rise
The perfumes that my soul desires.

Ah might I dance for ever, bent
Toward your bosom's clouded gleam,
And let the lilies' acrid scent
Withhold me in the world of dream!

Sonnet Macabre

I love you for the grief that lurks within
Your languid spirit, and because you wear
Corruption with a vague and childish air,
And with your beauty know the depths of sin;

Because shame cuts and holds you like a gin,
And virtue dies in you slain by despair,
Since evil has you tangled in its snare
And triumphs on the soul good cannot win.

I love you since you know remorse and tears,
And in your troubled loveliness appears
The spot of ancient crimes that writhe and hiss:

I love you for your hands that calm and bless,
The perfume of your sad and slow caress,
The avid poison of your subtle kiss.

White Lilies

Flowers rare and sweet I sent, whose delicate white
Should, grouping at her corsage, interlace
Their purity with her corrupted grace,
With the full throat and mouth of my delight.

Evil design! To see the pale flowers slight
The beauty of the worn and powdered face,
Mingling their costly virtue with the trace
Of ancient loves that live in time's despite.

How soon they died, poor blossoms! at her throat
Ere of the last valse died the last sad note
No more than love of her meant to endure,

For all the savour of her lips, the spice
Of her frail spirit steeped in cultured vice,
Gracefully bad and delicately impure!

Hothouse Flowers

I hate the flower of wood or common field.
I cannot love the primrose nor regret
The death of any shrinking violet,
Nor even the cultured garden's banal yield.

159

The silver lips of lilies virginal,
The full deep bosom of the enchanted rose
Please less than flowers glass-hid from frost and snows
For whom an alien heat makes festival.

I love those flowers reared by man's careful art,
Of heady scents and colors: strong of heart
Or weak that die beneath the touch of knife,

Some rich as sin and some as virtue pale,
And some as subtly infamous and frail
As she whose love still eats my soul and life.

ALAN STANLEY

Now Dies the Sun

Now dies the sun and all the sky is red
With his outflowing life blood; one by one
The sleepy flowers droop a languid head,—
      Now dies the sun.

Along the wall the slanting shadows run
And quiver through the golden iris-bed,
While warning birds proclaim that day is done.

Lo! the pale moon by gentle breezes led
Drifts like a wraith, ere night has yet begun,
All grows so hushed, the very world seems dead,—
      Now dies the sun.

A Night Club and a Valse

Draw back the curtains, let the dawn come in
And let new daylight mingle with the light
Of candles that have guttered through the night,
Of flaring gas-jets in this haunt of sin.

The sleepy orchestra. begins a tune,
'Tis the last valse and you with languid smile

Renew your well-worn witchery, and guile
Of eyes that 'neath their painted lashes swoon.

O how the music pulses, rises, calls,
On tremulous strings of ill-tuned violins,
Whispering of agonies and aching sins,
And a wild longing o'er my spirit falls;

For as like spectres we two move along
My mouth upon your mouth, the music seems
A memory exquisite of dying dreams
Which in my brain beats forth this dancing song.

Ah darling, daylight is not for us twain;
For us the darkness and the biting pain
Of love that hate becomes, yet yearning still
Drinks deep of passion, and may never fill
The aching void of longing. Come, once more
Let us glide swiftly o'er the polished floor
To the mad music of the Toréador.
And let our feet trip as with frenzy fired,
For both our hearts are breaking and so tired
That we would fain fall to a lasting sleep
With eyes so weary that they may not weep.
O that we two upon the last sweet strain
Might drift away! nor ever know again
Joy's cloying dulness, or sin's wearing pain.

G. F. MONKSHOOD

Léonie

Languid-lidded, motionless,
Curving like a leopardess
Curving with a feline grace
Before your bedroom fire.
Surely there's some sort of kin
Twixt the leopardess, whose skin
You now crouch on, and your form,
    Without, within.

Move your limbs: their lissomness
Rouse my senses listlessness,
Lift your languid-lidded eyes,
And let them catch the fire.
From your flame-shot silken hair
To your feet, unslippered, bare,
I possess you, leopardess,
    In this, your lair.

See, with hands of fearlessness,
I provoke your fierce caress—
Adding to your longing lips
The final touch that fires.
As you throb and undulate,
And your glorious eyes dilate,
I would lose all else on earth
    With you to mate.

AUBREY BEARDSLEY

The Three Musicians

Along the path that skirts the wood,
    The three musicians wend their way,
Pleased with their thoughts, each other's mood,
    Franz Himmel's latest roundelay,
The morning's work, a new-found theme, their breakfast
    and the summer day.

One's a soprano, lightly frocked
    In cool, white muslin that just shows
Her brown silk stockings gaily clocked,
    Plump arms and elbows tipped with rose,
And frills of petticoats and things, and outlines as the
    warm wind blows.

Beside her a slim, gracious boy
    Hastens to mend her tresses' fall,
And dies her favour to enjoy,
    And dies for réclame and recall
At Paris and St. Petersburg, Vienna and St. James's Hall.

The third's a Polish Pianist
    With big engagements everywhere,
A light heart and an iron wrist,

And shocks and shoals of yellow hair,
And fingers that can trill on sixths and fill beginners with
    despair.

    The three musicians stroll along
        And pluck the ears of ripened corn,
    Break into odds and ends of song,
        And mock the woods with Siegfried's horn,
And fill the air with Gluck, and fill the tweeded tourist's
    soul with scorn.

    The Polish genius lags behind,
        And, with some poppies in his hand,
    Picks out the strings and wood and wind
        Of an imaginary band,
Enchanted that for once his men obey his beat and
    understand.

    The charming cantatrice reclines
        And rests a moment where she sees
    Her chateau's roof that hotly shines
        Amid the dusky summer trees,
And fans herself, half shuts her eyes, and smoothes the
    frock about her knees.

    The gracious boy is at her feet,
        And weighs his courage with his chance;
    His fears soon melt in noon-day heat.
        The tourist gives a furious glance,
Red as his guide-book grows, moves on, and offers up a
    prayer for France.

J. F. BLOXAM

A Summer Hour

Love tarried for a moment on his way,
Against my cheek his curly head he lay;
He said that he would never leave my breast
If I would give him what I valued best.
Mine arms went out to greet him then and there,
What heart had I to cast out one so fair?

He whispered that his little feet were sore,
He was so weary he could go no more,
He showed the wounds upon his tender flesh,
And, as he whispered, bound me in his mesh.
He whispered in mine ear his piteous tale,
What heart had I to cast out one so frail?

I kissed his little hands, his lips, his hair,
And kissing gave my soul into his care,
Love laughed a little, like a child at play,—
"Regretted that he could no longer stay,
He had so many things to do to-day,"—
Another moment Love was far away.

BENJAMIN DE CASSERES

Moth-Terror

I have killed the moth flying around my night-light;
    wingless and dead it lies upon the floor.
(O who will kill the great Time-Moth that eats holes in my
    soul and that burrows in and through my secretest veils!)
My will against its will, and no more will it fly at my
    night-light or be hidden behind the curtains that swing
    in the winds.
(But O who will shatter the Change-Moth that leaves me
    in rags—-tattered old tapestries that swing in the winds
    that blow out of Chaos!)
Night-Moth, Change-Moth, Time-Moth, eaters of dreams
    and of me!

Magical Night

My withered dreams rebloomed last night,
And to the strains of a triumphal march
Played on the keys of the hours
By the Blind Beethoven of the Stars
I wandered again
With Lilith and Eve and Cain and Orpheus
Through the elf-haunted gardens of my youth.

The Haunted House

My brain is a tropical forest,
Dark and sinister,
In whose branches thoughts dart and play
Like crimson scarabees—
A sea of phosphorescent light
In which images sport like flying fish.
A garden, too,
Wherein walk sadic Christs
And Neros that are Paraclete—
A seraglio peopled with scarlet angels
Who chant their hymns of passion
To the cataleptic Sultan of the Skies.

My brain is a chariot of sun-motes
Drawn by two great butterflies
Caught by Moon-Titans,
Who carry me past the sparkling sweat-beads
On the face of the celestial Ethiope
And the multi-billioned infusoria
Who pullulate in their depths
To the solemn solitudes of the Nirvana of fairies
Who drowse forever on the Golden Thigh of
Pythagoras.

My brain! My brain!
A star exiled from Space
To the Siberia of my skull
Without reprieve!

OLIVE CUSTANCE

A Dream

I dreamed we walked together, you and I,
Along a white and lonely road, that went
I know not where . . . and we were well content.
Our laughter was untroubled as the sky,
And all our talk was delicate and shy,
Though in that cage of words wild thoughts were pent
Like prisoned birds that some sweet accident
Might yet release to sing again, and fly.
We passed between long lines of poplar trees . . .
Where, summer comrades gay and debonair,
The south wind and the sunlight danced . . . you smiled,
With great glad eyes, as bright as summer seas,
To feel their twinkling fingers in your hair . .
And then you kissed me, quickly, like a child!

Shadow-Nets

When I was wandering on the Downs to-day
I saw the pine-woods sleeping in the sun . . .
For they were tired of weaving shadow-nets—
Weaving all day in vain . . . in vain . . . in vain . . .
Pale phantom nets to snare the golden sun!
And then I thought of how the poets weave
With shadowy words their cunning nets of song,
Hoping to catch, at last, a shining dream!

HELEN HAY WHITNEY

A Dream in Fever

A vast screen of unequal downward lines,
An orange purple halo 'round the rain,
Twists from a space whose very size is pain.
Here in this vortex day with night combines;
Ruby and Emerald glint their blazing spines;
Closing and smothering, wheels a brazen main,
A shuddering sea of silence; in its train
A thought—a cry, whose snake fear trembling twines
Around above alive yet uttered not;
But my heart hears and shrieking dies of dread,
Then soaring breaks its bands and o'er the rim
White winged it rends the dark with jagged blot,
Glimpsing the iris gateway barred ahead,
And, gazing thro', the eyes of cherubim.

The Forgiveness

If I might see you dead, Beloved—dead—
    Your false eyes closed forever to the light,
    Your false smile stilled upon my aching sight;
If I might know that nevermore your head,
Cruelly fair, could lie upon the bed

Of my torn heart; if I beheld the night
Free from your living thought—ah! if I might,
Then could my desolate soul be comforted.

For this is worst of all the woes you gave—
My heart may not forgive. The tired years go
And leave the great love weeping for a grave,
Scorned and unburied, 'neath the open sky.
I could not love you less, to see you so.
Loving you more, I might forgive—and die.

Flowers of Ice

The lights within the ice-floes are our flowers,
Lily and daffodil and violet.
Beneath these monstrous suns that never set
Tremble soft rainbows, young as Earth's first hours,
Ancient as Time. No balm of gentle showers
Make for their growth; for them, gigantic, met
The immemorial ice and sun, to get
Such blossoms—pledge of Beauty's bravest powers.

Violet and pale grass-green, the Spring-time dies
In the soft South. To us, in this grim world,
Daring with frozen heart and tearless eyes
The North's white sanctity, Fate idly throws
These alms—a deathless Spring of ice enfurled,
And over all, far flung, the sunset rose.

To a Moth

Spirit of evil, heavily flying, turning,
    Dropping to earth,
Caught to the light, with brown wings torn and burning,
    Whence was your birth?

Was there a cause that, ceaselessly turning, flying,
    Drew you from night?
All that we know is this—the aimless dying,
Killed by the light.

Evil the star that led you, spirit of evil,
    Out of your dark,
Breeding desire that conquers us, man and devil—
    Passion's red spark.

The Monk in His Garden

The air is heavy with a mist of spice,
    Vervain and agrimony, clove and rue,
Have I not paid, have I not paid the price?
    How shall these tempters torture me anew?

I close my eyes and dream the incense drifts
    Over the monstrance, and the acolyte
Swings the gold censer. Then the vision lifts:
    I know the poisonous joys I have to fight.

Day with its flowers and yellow butterflies,
    Holds for my heart no pain, the wind is free

That blows upon my garden from far skies,
   Yet may I hold it in white chastity.

But night!—and the still air!—Ah, God above,
   Have I the strength to wage thy war anew?
Blot out my senses or I die for love,—
   Vervain and agrimony, clove and rue!

An Impressionist Picture

"How do you do," I said; the yellow coat
   She wore was like a golden serpent's skin.
   I took her white gloved hand, my voice grew thin
As tho' her hand were tight about my throat.
The air was green with heat, a flaccid note
   I did not fail to see, for heat might win
   My cause; her weary soul looked from within
And saw the white sails flapping on my boat.

"Coolness and rest" my eyes were whispering,
   In Isles where morn grows never afternoon,
   Where Passion buds forever with the Spring,
   Nor wanes with shifting tides of sea and moon,
But—"How are you?" she said, and that was all,
And tho' she smiled, she passed beyond recall.

ALEISTER CROWLEY

At Kiel

Oh, the white flame of limbs in dusky air,
  The furnace of thy great grey eyes on me
  Turned till I shudder. Darkness on the sea,
And wan ghost-lights are flickering everywhere
So that the world is ghastly. But within
  Where we two cling together, and hot kisses
  Stray to and fro amid the wildernesses
Of swart curled locks! I deem it a sweet sin,
So sweet that fires of hell have no more power
  On body and soul to quench the lustrous flame
Of that desire that burns between us twain.
What is Eternity, seeing we hold this hour
  For all the lusts and luxuries of shame?
Heaven is well lost for this surpassing gain.

Necrophilia

Void of the ecstasies of Art
  It were in life to have lain by thee,
  And felt thy kisses rain on me,
And the hot beating of thy heart,

When thy warm sweat should leave me cold,
    And my worn soul find out no bliss
    In the obscenities I kiss,
And the things shameful that I hold.

My nostrils sniff the luxury
    Of flesh decaying, bowels torn
    Of festive worms, like Venus, born
Of entrails foaming like the sea.

Yea, thou art dead. Thy buttocks now
    Are swan-soft, and thou sweatest not;
    And hast a strange desire begot
In me, to lick thy bloody brow;

To gnaw thy hollow cheeks, and pull
    Thy lustful tongue from out its sheath;
    To wallow in the bowels of death,
And rip thy belly, and fill full

My hands with all putridities;
    To chew thy dainty testicles;
    To revel with the worms in Hell's
Delight in such obscenities;

To pour within thine heart the seed
    Mingled with poisonous discharge
    From a swollen gland, inflamed and large
With gonorrhoea's delicious breed;

To probe thy belly, and to drink
    The godless fluids, and the pool

Of rank putrescence from the stool
Thy hanged corpse gave, whose luscious stink

Excites these songs sublime. The rod
    Gains new desire; dive, howl, cling, suck,
    Rave, shriek, and chew; excite the fuck,
Hold me, I come! I'm dead! My God!

Sleeping in Carthage

The month of thirst is ended. From the lips
That hide their blushes in the golden wood
A fervent fountain amorously slips,
The dainty rivers of thy luscious blood;
Red streams of sweet nepenthe that eclipse
The milder nectar that the gods hold good—
How my dry throat, held hard between thy hips,
Shall drain the moon-wrought flow of womanhood!

Divinest token of sterility,
Strange barren fountain blushing from the womb,
Like to an echo of Augustan gloom
When all men drank this wine; it maddens me
With yearnings after new divinity,
Prize of thy draught, somewhere beyond the tomb.

DAVID PARK BARNITZ

Opium

Naught is more sweet than gently to let dream
The pallid flower of life asleep alway;
Where the dim censer sends up far from day
Unceasingly its still-ascending stream,

O where the air winds its myrrh-scented steam
About thy naked body's disarray,
Shall not today's gold to thy shut eyes seem
Born and forgot in the dead ages gray?

Sunk from life's mournful loud processional,
For thee shall not with high uplifted urn
The Night pour out dreams that awake and say,

—We were, O pallid maiden vesperal,
Before the world; we also in our turn
By the vain morning gold scatter'd away.

Mummy

Thou art at last made perfect; from the estate
Of mushy life Death hath thee petrified.
The soft the flowing and the putrified
That made thee up, is by that artist great

Now crystalliz'd unto a changeless state.
That thing thou walkedst, nos'd and ear'd and eyed,
Eternally severely doth abide,
Sunk from the bands of them that drank and ate.

Green mummies walk above thy walled gloom,
Unripen'd mummies; they intemperate
Seek in life's beauty their high-crowned doom

In vain. But thee no passion doth illume
Stiff in the musked darkness of the tomb
Hard in stiff bands of red and nacarat.

Ennui

I sat in tall Gomorrah on a day,
Boring myself with solitude and dreams,
When, like strange priests, with sacerdotal tread,
The seven mortal sins, in rich array,

Came in and knelt: one old, and weak, and gray,
One that was shrouded like a person dead,
And one whose robes cast reddish-purple gleams
Upon her scornful face at peace alway.

They swung before me amschirs of strange gold,
And one most beautiful began to pray,
Dreamily garmented in pallid blue.

But I said only—I have dream'd of you.
Naught really is; all things are very old,
And very foolish. Please to go away.

Ashtoreth

In thy blue pallid gown that shimmereth
So pale thou standest in the wan moonlight,
Where the gold censer near thy body white
Wraps thee around with its perfumed breath;

So wan thy high tiara glimmereth
Above thy mystical far eyes of light,
Thou seemest some dead goddess of the night,
O starry love, O changeless Ashtoreth.

Pallid thou standest in thy divinity,
Like some moon-idol of the buried time,
Before whose face priests sing in solemn chime.

So I prostrate before thy deity,
Unto thy face have solemn praises sung,
And in my hands a golden censer swung.

Miserrimus

In the last hopeless depth of hell's dark tomb
Wherein I sit for aye with bowed head
In anguish and great sorrow buried
Where never sun the blackness doth illume,

I saw pass by me through the bitter gloom
All them whom life with deepest grief hath fed,
Whom also here among the hopeless dead
Through hell pursueth maniac, gnashing doom.

Me there forever crusht to hopeless stone
They passt by, all the damn'd; they shall not know
Through all eternity but only woe,
Now hear no sound but sound of them that groan.

And unto me that sat than these more low,
These seem'd like happy gods that heaven own;
They past away; and there in hell alone
My heart took up again its ancient woe.

The Grotesques

I.

I saw a dead corpse lying in a tomb,
Long buried and rotten to the core;
Behold this corpse shall know not evermore
Aught that may be outside its wormy room;

It lies uncover'd in the pesty gloom,
Eyeless and earless, on the charnel-floor,
While in its nameless corpse the wormlets hoar
Make in its suppurated brain their room.

And in that charnel that no lights illume,
It shriek'd of things that lay outside its door;
And while the still worms through its soft heart bore,

It lay and reason'd of the ways of doom,
And in its head thoughts mov'd as in a womb;
And in its heart the worms lie evermore.

II.

I saw a dead corpse in a haughty car,
Whom in a high tomb phantom horses bore,
Aye to and fro upon the scatter'd floor;
His dead eyes star'd as though they look'd afar,

His gold wheels myriad perish'd souls did mar,
While through his flesh the ravenous wormlets tore;
He in whose eyes the worm was conqueror,
Held his high head unmoved like a star.

And as with loud sound and reverberant jar,
And as with splash of crusht flesh and dull roar,
The death-car thunder'd past the tomb-walls hoar,

Within those dead dominions the dead tsar
Receiv'd his plaudits where dead bodies are;
And in his heart the worms lie evermore.

III.

I saw a dead corpse making a strange cry,
With dead feet planted on a high tomb's floor;
The dead stand round, with faces that implore;
His dead hands bless them, stretched forth on high.

—And art them God? and art them majesty?—
And art thou he whom all the dead adore?—

And art thou he that hath the skies in store?—
Nay, nay, dead dust, dead dust, and vanity.

And wouldst thou rise up to the lighted sky?—
Nay, nay, thy limbs are rotten on the floor;
Thou shalt not out from thy polluted sty;

Thou wouldst become divinity once more,
Thou dreamest of splendour that shall never die;
And in thy heart the worms lie evermore.

IV.

I saw a dead corpse lying on the floor
Of a tomb; worms were in its woman's head,
Its black flesh lay about it shred on shred,
And the dead things slept in its bosom hoar.

And evermore inside that loathed door,
It turn'd itself as one upon a bed,
It turn'd itself as one whom sleep hath fled,
As one that the sweet pangs of passion bore.

And from its passionate mouth's corrupted sore,
And from its lips that are no longer red,
Came forth love's accents; and it spake, and said.

—The Pleiades and night's noon-hours are o'er,
And I am left alone in wearyhead.
And in its heart the worms lie evermore.

T. H. T. CASE

Lesbia

Let us live and love, my Lesbia,
Heeding not the sage's cry,
As it girds across the ages,
"All that is, is Vanity."

Suns may see another dawning,
Rest them for another light,
When our life sets, there remaineth
Deepening shades of dawnless night.

Night! Ah drown the word's dark boding
In a kiss's crestless wave,
That upon a bridge of kisses,
We may dance across the grave.

The Decadent

I stood beside the flower-beds,
    Watching the petals fall;
One waited there beside me,
    Who plucked them all.

Idly the petals fluttered,
    Flaunting their painted pride;
Sweetened the air a moment,
    Quivered, and died.

I watched the petals falling
    Till the lilies lay forlorn,
And the roses' ruined splendour
    Bared the sharp thorn.

And I turned to her that shred them
    (Deft-handed, lissome, she),
And I saw her name upon her brow:
    "Perversity."

She has robbed my life of roses,
    No more my lilies blow;
And still she waits beside me—
    She may not go.

But now her hands have drawn me
    To the wilderness apart.
No more she shreds the roses:
    She shreds my heart.

Are my red roses fallen?
    My queenly lilies dead?
The lilies were not queenly
    Nor the roses red.

SAROJINI NAIDU

Eastern Dancers

Eyes ravished with rapture, celestially panting, what
    passionate spirits aflaming with fire
Drink deep of the hush of the hyacinth heavens that
    glimmer around them in fountains of light?
O wild and entrancing the strain of keen music that
    cleaveth the stars like a wail of desire,
And beautiful dancers with Houri-like faces bewitch the
    voluptuous watches of Night.
The scents of red roses and sandalwood flutter and die in
    the maze of their gem-tangled hair,
And smiles are entwining like magical serpents the poppies
    of lips that are opiate-sweet,
Their glittering garments of purple are burning like
    tremulous dawns in the quivering air,
And exquisite, subtle and slow are the tinkle and tread of
    their rhythmical slumber-soft feet.
Now silent, now singing and swaying and swinging, like
    blossoms that bend to the breezes or showers,
Now wantonly winding, they flash, now they falter, and
    lingering languish in radiant choir,
Their jewel-bright arms and warm, wavering, lily-long
    fingers enchant thro' the summer-swift hours,
Eyes ravished with rapture, celestially panting, their
    passionate spirits aflaming with fire.

MONTAGUE SUMMERS

To a Dead Acolyte

See! I will place them there
To crown thine endless rest,
A sheaf of lilies fair
Upon thy weary breast.
They nestle 'mid thy gilded hair,
Flowers, which but yesternoon
Were blithe with sunlit life, now swoon
Exhaling their last fragrant breath
In the wan room of death.

Lilies strown about thy head
Content to die sith thou art dead.
Thy cheek is whiter than their glow
Of dim perfection, and thy brow
More candid than the new fallen snow.
Thou art at peace and sleepest now.

Thy lips are still and pale,
Pale from Death's icy kiss.
The radiance of thine wondrous eyes
No more shall flame with earthly bliss.
For thou hast seen beyond the veil
The mysteries of God, whilst we
With many a doubt and mad surmise
Peer wonderingly.

No more thy reverent accents, sweet,
Shall answer at the Mass,
No more thy gentle flower-like feet
About the Altar pass.
Thou wast so near to God,
Thou couldst no nearer be,
Save this one way alone,
Thy Lover chose for thee.

Hush! Thou art asleep.
Ah, yes, 'tis better so.
Shall we impatient weep
That thou wast bidden go?
Dear, let me look once more
Upon thine innocence,
With joy let me adore,
Since unstained love and trust were thine,
That thou hast never known the pain
The vague regret when boyish dreams
Dissolve, and all is vain.

WALTER DE CASSERES

Voiceless

I feel unuttered melodies,
I tread the far world-dotted way,
I strive in vain to touch the keys
That lead the soul toward the skies—
The music deep within me dies
Nor sees the blessed light of day.

My wild heart roams beyond the stars,
But only knows a plaintive wail,
While something still within me bars
The dreams from being more than sighs—
The music deep within me dies
And leaves my grief an untold tale.

The Battle of the Passions

From out of the depths of the night,
A blood-red battalion they come,
They laugh, for with them lies the might,
And they know we shall have to succumb,

Heart-eating, venomous worms,
Brain-burning, horrible things,

That make the heart shudder and pale
And shatter the soul with their stings.

Silently onward they press,
And, writhing around and beneath,
They sting and they pierce with their fangs
And bite with their terrible teeth.

Soon—soon the dread battle is over,
But the conquerors never retire,
And ever are watchful and wakeful
And ever are scourging with fire.

But now draweth near the avengers,
The invincible Army of Death—
They charge with the rush of a whirlwind
And scatter the worms with their breath.

And the sound of the wearisome struggle
And the thought of that terrible fight
Pass on as a dream that the devils
Have whispered to us in the night.

The Suicide

He sought for things he could not find,
He hunted through the weary years,
The path was watered by his tears,
And Life was cold, though Death was kind.

He sought for love in a woman's heart,
For truth within a woman's eyes—
He sought for truth where falsehood lies
And looked for love where love is not.

He cried to God, but He was dead;
To her, but she did not reply;
He thought perhaps 'twere best to die,
His dreams forever left unsaid.

NORA MAY FRENCH

Vivisection

We saw unpitying skill
  In curious hands put living flesh apart,
 Till, bare and terrible, the tiny heart
Pulsed, and was still.

We saw Grief's sudden knife
  Strip through the pleasant flesh of soul-disguise—
 Lay for a second's space before our eyes
A naked life.

Rebuke

The tortured river-banks, the toiling piers—
  I walked thereby as older grew the day,
And sick with sorry clamor in mine ears,
  Heart-weary turned my steps and went my way.

"O place full-voiced of wretchedness!" I cried.
  (The sun had set, the dusk was closing in)
"O place where laboring Life goes heavy-eyed,
  Compound of grime and discord, strife and sin!"

I turned me back, and lo, a miracle!
    For misty violet lay along the land.
The shining river in mysterious spell
    (Divinely touched by some transmuting hand).

A path of wonder was, and on it stirred,
    (Black-shaped, and jeweled with a crimson spark)
A ship that slowly moved; and, faintly heard,
    A cheery song rose blithely to the dark.

The Panther Woman

I face the tranquil day with tranquil eyes
On high sea-hills my cheeks are cold with mist,
In white foam-fingers quick desire dies.

Dies as a strangled bird the wave has torn—
Ay, drowns and dies this winged desire of mine
In white sea fingers of the tidal morn.

But I would kill the restless silken night
And I would still the wings that beat the dark,
And grasp the little throat of heart-delight,

And drown the savage will that understands
How love would laugh to clasp your bending head,
How love would hold your face in her two hands,

How love would press your angry lips apart,
And leave the willful bruising of her kiss
In the sweet satin flesh above your heart.

VICTOR BENJAMIN NEUBURG

The Cauldron

To Ethel Archer

I was born when a witch
Spread her withered hands over a blaze,
   With a big hazel-switch
   With notches for days,
With notches for days.
And slimy and rich
   Her ugly voice prays:
By God! I was there with the witch!

What matter to me
If the sun be at war with the sea?
   Will they drench me or burn?
   I was born in the heart of an urn
When the gold was all fled;
And they thought I was dead
Before birth, but I sped
   Forth, forth from the fire
   And lo! with desire
I escaped, and I roam
At will from my home.

They call me, and lo!
Why should I go?
They feed me with gold;
They are withered and old,
For I suck and I suck,
And they give me good luck.

Lo! I am one with the air,
For air is my blood and red fire is my hair,
And the wind is my lair.
    And they draw me with thought,
    For of air am I wrought.
They call me, and then
I flee among men,
    And madness and rust
    And the music of dust
I give them, and they,
    With the fury of trust,
    Feed me with flame of desire and bright lust!
And I conquer the day,
And I float, and I float, and I float far away.

EDMUND JOHN

Songe d'Ennui

. . . Dreams, always dreams and weariness;
Paths of dead roses where I go
To rid myself of the hot noontide's dreariness:
Scents of malmaison from a year ago.

Alleys of Autumn leaves and flowers,
Cypress and sea-lavender around,
And blossoms weary with the memory of past hours
Lie low and broken on the reed-grown ground.

The tangled foliage has grown
Upon this grave of passions dead,
Which sleeps beside the path whereon I walk alone
Within this silent garden perfuméd.

Here, far since, where the green moss clings,
Love lay, and looked into my eyes,
Deep, long; then sighing, fled to where the mavis sings,
And in his place the breath of Autumn lies.

—Shadows, pearl-pale, of rose and grey,
Of faded green, of weariness that seems
To have crept here with me far from the heavy day,
Into this path of roses and still dreams.

Nocturne

To R—— L——

No sound except a fitful minor chord
Of moonlight on the leaves, and odours stored
By flowers at noon from children's scented hair,
And incense from the earth swift-kissed by rain,
And lilies and narcissi, and the pain
Of my wild heart in knowing you are there.

Night's deep green colours, passionate and grave,
Sing through this shadowy rhododendron cave,
Like funeral music in the tomb of Love.
No light is here; though on the fragrant flowers,
From which the rain-drops count the dying hours,
The moon shines from the broken clouds above.

But darkness cannot hide your face from me,
For were I dead my closed, still eyes would see
Its narrow oval, and the red, dark mouth
With that slight touch of cruelty that is spent
In passionate lines and crimson, like the scent
Of champak and strange perfumes from the South.

Ah! you are near me—and your wild eyes seem
Like deep, dark pools where lonely mountains dream,
And all the sorrow of your fragrant breath,
The night of your dark hair, have taught me this,
—That I will know to-night the wild hard kiss
That from your lips shall crown my love with death.

Litany of the Seven Devils

To M. C. B.

There are Seven Devils in my heart,
That sleep through wintry days, but in the nights of June
Pour forth their vials before the half-veiled violet moon,
And lave their limbs with incense sweet and curious,
And fling red roses where white lilies had been strewn.

There are Seven Devils in my heart
And when one stirs and wakes, I start, and feel soft-pressed
The delicate satin body slide upwards o'er my breast,
Veiling my eyes and lips with perfume sensuous,
Full of elusive music and a strange unrest.

There are Seven Devils in my heart
And one is lithe and dark and warm, with shining eyes
Of deep imaginings, and subtle hands like sighs
That fall upon my skin, and poignant finger-tips
That touch my soul to madness bright that crucifies.

There are Seven Devils in my heart;
One has a voice like flutes entwined with jessamine,
That haunts the lotus-paths my strange thoughts wander in
And stirs the summer aisles of moonlit odorous flowers,
Which lead to the pale temple of forbidden sin.

There are Seven Devils in my heart;
And one is young and agile, with limbs slim and bare
And scented with the lure of youth, and eyes that snare
With the frail call of dawn, and wayward heart wound round
By delicate wickedness like some half-wanton prayer.

There are Seven Devils in my heart;
One with the burning hands of God, and words that beat
With lordship o'er men's souls and bodies—power sweet
And terrible, evil and good, that can call forth
Children and flowers of Spring from Winter's winding-sheet.

There are Seven Devils in my heart;
And one, with my own eyes and voice from the lost years,
Holds up an opal mirror set with pearls like tears,
And dreams my own dead dreams; and my maimed hopes
    he knows,
And sees each deed, and all the words I say he hears.

There are Seven Devils in my heart;
And one, upon whose forehead gleams a wondrous name,
With ivory limbs and kissed feet shod with lambent flame,
Calls with gold wings toward the unattainable,
And bids me trample heaven and hell, honour and shame.

There are Seven Devils in my heart
And one there is who stands upon the eastern slope
At dawn, when Day flings off Night's purple cope.
Him most of all I fear; master of pain is he;
His eyes are sad, his path a circle, and his name is Hope.

There are Seven Devils in my heart,
    With strange elusive eyes,
    And sensuous lips, and sighs
    Of night, and tears which rise
From bitter memories that smart.
Are they Seven Devils set apart
    Or is it some disguise
Of Angels who shall soon depart?

JAMES ELROY FLECKER

Tenebris Interlucentem

A linnet who had lost her way
Sang on a blackened bough in Hell,
Till all the ghosts remembered well
The trees, the wind, the golden day.
At last they knew that they had died
When they heard music in that land,
And someone there stole forth a hand
To draw a brother to his side.

The Translator and the Children

While I translated Baudelaire,
Children were playing out in the air.
Turning to watch, I saw the light
That made their clothes and faces bright.
I heard the tune they meant to sing
As they kept dancing in a ring;
But I could not forget my book,
And thought of men whose faces shook
When babies passed them with a look.

They are as terrible as death,
Those children in the road beneath.
Their witless chatter is more dread
Than voices in a madman's head:
Their dance more awful and inspired,
Because their feet are never tired,
Than silent revel with soft sound
Of pipes, on consecrated ground,
When all the ghosts go round and round.

November Eves

November Evenings! Damp and still
They used to cloak Leckhampton hill,
And lie down close on the grey plain,
And dim the dripping window-pane,
And send queer winds like Harlequins
That seized our elms for violins
And struck a note so sharp and low
Even a child could feel the woe.

Now fire chased shadow round the room;
Tables and chairs grew vast in gloom:
We crept about like mice, while Nurse
Sat mending, solemn as a hearse,
And even our unlearned eyes
Half closed with choking memories.

Is it the mist or the dead leaves,
Or the dead men—November eves?

ABOUT THE AUTHORS

DOUGLAS AINSLIE (1865-1948) was a Scottish poet, translator, and diplomat, who was born in Paris but educated in England. He was a contributor to *The Yellow Book* and friends with many noteworthy figures associated with that journal, including Oscar Wilde and Aubrey Beardsley. Among his translations is *Of Dandyism and of George Brummell* (1897), by Jules Barbey d'Aurevilly. "The Death of Verlaine" and "Her Colours" originally appeared in the April 1897 issue of *The Yellow Book*, while "The Vampire and the Dove" is taken from *Mirage* (1911).

HENRY WILLARD AUSTIN (1858-1912) was a contributor of poetry to many of the important, and unimportant, North American periodicals of his day, including the Boston based *The Nationalist*, which he edited, and which under his guidance published the work of Stuart Merrill. "Une Fleur du Mal" is taken from Austin's collection *Vagabond Verses* (1890).

JOHN BARLAS (1860-1914), who wrote under the pseudonym of "Evelyn Douglas," was born in Burma, the son of a successful merchant, and educated in Oxford, where he became close friends with Oscar Wilde. Between 1884-1893 he published eight collections of poetry, all of which remained in obscurity. After exhausting most of his inheritance, he lived by teaching, and became involved in anarchist and socialist circles. In 1887, on Bloody Sunday, he was struck in the head with a police truncheon while protesting. On the last day of the year 1891, he was arrested after discharging a revolver three times at the House of Commons, and was subsequently bailed out by Wilde. The final third of his life was spent in a mental institution in Scotland. "Oblivion" is taken from *Holy of Holies: Confessions of an Anarchist* (1897); "Beauty's Anadems," "The Cat-Lady" and "Terrible Love" are all three taken from the postumously published *Yew-Leaf and Lotus-Petal: Sonnets* (1935); the "Dedicatory Sonnet" is from *The Queen of the Hid Isle* (1885).

DAVID PARK BARNITZ (1878-1901), was an American poet who, before perishing at a young age, published anonymously a single volume dedicated to the memory of Charles Baudelaire, *The Book of Jade* (1901), from which all six items in the present collection are taken.

"LOUIS BARSAC" was the pseudonym of the journalist and novelist Ernest James Oldmeadow (1867-1949). Under his true name he was editor first of the London *Musical Times*, and subsequently the Catholic periodical the *Tablet*, and also published several novels, including *The North Sea Bubble: A Fantasia* (1906). The Barsac pseudonym seems to have been used exclusively for the poetry which dominated the early part of his career, much of which was collected together in the volume *Shadows and Fireflies: A Book of Verse* (1898), from which "A Grey Morning," "The Poppies," "Did He Know?" and "Without Form and Void" were taken; "Vision" first appeared in the magazine *The Dome* in 1897.

AUBREY BEARDSLEY (1872-1898) was the leading illustrator of the Decadent style in England and the co-founder of both *The Yellow Book* and the *The Savoy*, the January 1896 issue of the latter publication being where "The Three Musicians" first appeared.

MATHILDE BLIND (1841-1896) was born in Mannheim, Germany, the daughter of the banker Jacob Abraham Cohen and his wife, whose maiden name was Friederike Ettlinger. Her father died in 1848 and her mother, the same year, remarried the German revolutionist and writer Karl Blind. In 1852 the family immigrated to London where Blind attended the Ladies' Institute. After initially publishing poetry under the pseudonym "Claude Lake," she began publishing extensively under her own name, not only poetry, but also essays, biographies, and a novel, emerging as one of the most important aesthetic voices of her day. "A Winter Landscape" is taken from *The Ascent of Man* (1898); "The Forest Pool" is taken from *Birds of Passage: Songs of the Orient and Occident* (1895); "Despair" is taken from *The Prophecy of St. Oran and Other Poems* (1881).

J. F. BLOXAM (1873-1928), a friend of George Ives and Alfred Douglas, was the editor of the sole issue of *The Chameleon*, which included a contribution by Alfred Douglas and another by Oscar Wilde, which was submitted at Douglas' request, to the later dismay of Wilde, since the magazine was used as "evidence" of Wilde's "unnatural habits" in the 1895 trials held against him. Bloxam afterwards became an ordained priest. "A Summer Hour" is taken from the October 1894 issue of *The Artist*, where it appeared under the pseudonym of "Bertram Lawrence."

CHRISTOPHER JOHN BRENNAN (1870-1932) was an Australian poet, scholar and literary critic. Heavily influenced by the writing of Mallarmé, whom he corresponded with and who praised his work, Brennan was possibly Australia's only true heir to the Symbolist Movement. "Nox Marmorea" originally appeared in the University of Sydney undergraduate journal *Hermes* in 1902.

HORATIO F. BROWN (1854-1926) was born in Nice, raised in Scotland, educated in England, and spent much of his life in Venice, writing about the lagoons, hanging out with gondoliers, and associating with such people as Frederick Rolfe and John Addington Symonds, who made him his literary executor. "'Bored': At a London Music" is taken from his collection *Drift* (1900).

T. H. T. CASE is an author of which little today is known. From information found in old journals, he seems to have been an admirer of Ernest Dowson, but otherwise the only evidence that can be gleaned as to his life and personality is from his two volumes of poetry, *Verses* (1905), from which "Lesbia" is taken, and *Songs and Poems* (1907) from which "The Decadent" has been extracted.

BENJAMIN DE CASSERES (1873-1945) was born in Philadelphia and worked as a journalist there, in New York, and in Mexico City. He wrote numerous books and pamphlets, many of which were heavily infused with Decadent themes. "Moth-Terror" is taken from *The Shadow-Eater* (1917), while "Magical Night" and "The Haunted House" are both taken from *Black Suns* (1936).

WALTER DE CASSERES (1881-1900), the younger brother of Benjamin De Casseres, committed suicide at the age of eighteen by jumping into the Delaware River. His single book of poetry *The Sublime Boy* (1926), posthumously published by his brother, is the source for the three pieces in the present volume.

ALEISTER CROWLEY (1875-1947), though primarily famous for being an English occultist, was also a keen practitioner of the Decadent poem, giving full evidence of this in his book *White Stains* (1898), from which all three items in the present anthology are taken.

OLIVE CUSTANCE (1874-1944), known also as Lady Alfred Douglas, was one of the important poets of the 1890s, having from an early age formed friendships with many of the principal Decadent poets of the day, including Renée Vivien, the latter recounting their relationship in her novel *Une femme m'apparut*. Despite having relationships with both Vivien and Natalie Clifford Barney, Custance married Lord Alfred Douglas in 1901. She was a regular contributor to *The Yellow Book* and produced four volumes of verse. "A Dream" is taken from *The Blue Bird* (1905); "Shadow-Nets" originally appeared in the March 23, 1907 issue of *The Academy*.

JOHN DAVIDSON (1857-1909) was a Scottish man of letters and member of the Rhymers' Club, best known for his poetry. A contributor of *The Yellow Book* and the writer of the flagellation novel *A Full and True Account of the Wonderful Mission of Earl Lavender*, which had a frontispiece by Aubrey Beardsley, Davidson skirted the perimeters of the English Decadent scene. "Holiday" is taken from *Holiday and Other Poems: With a Note on Poetry* (1906).

LORD ALFRED DOUGLAS (1870-1945), while at Oxford, edited the Decadent-leaning undergraduate journal, *The Spirit Lamp*, which published contributions by Oscar Wilde, with whom he had a close relationship, to the disgust of Douglas's father, which caused the public scandal that eventually led to Wilde's imprisonment. Douglas married Olive Custance and eventually converted to Catholicism. "Two Loves" and "In Praise of Shame" both originally appeared in the December 1894 issue of *The Chameleon*, while "Impressions de Nuit" and "The Sphinx" are taken from *The City of the Soul* (1899).

ERNEST DOWSON (1867-1900) was a member of the Rhymers' Club, and one of the key writers of the English Decadent Movement. He collaborated on two novels with Arthur Moore, and wrote several volumes of his own prose, but it is for his exquisite poetry that he is best remembered. "Non Sum Qualis Eram Bonae Sub Regno Cynarae" originally appeared in *The Second Book of the Rhymer's Club* (1894), while "Dregs" is taken from *Decorations in Verse and Prose* (1899).

LADY ALIX EGERTON (1870-1932), daughter of the author Charles Granville, the 3rd Earl of Ellesmere, was a poet, playwright, and Milton scholar, who contributed to a number of the journals of her day, most notably *The Green Sheaf*. "Phantoms" is taken from *The Lady of the Scarlet Shoes and Other Verses* (1903).

HAVELOCK ELLIS (1859-1939) was an English physician best remembered for his multi-volume series of books titled *Studies in the Psychology of Sex* (1897-1928). He contributed articles to *The Savoy*, included a marvellous essay on Huysmans in his *Affirmations* (1915), and, though certainly not a prolific poet, did produce a small amount of verse. "Schubert's Symphony in B Minor" originally appeared in the January 12, 1884 issue of *The Academy*.

JAMES ELROY FLECKER (1884-1915) was a London-born writer who excelled in many forms, producing fiction, dramas, and a number of volumes of verse, much of it Decadent. He died in Davos, Switzerland, of tuberculosis, at the age of thirty. "Tenebris Interlucentem" originally appeared in the Jun 4, 1910 issue of *The Living Age*, while "The Translator and the Children" is taken from *The Bridge of Fire* (1907), and "November Eves" from *The Old Ships* (1915).

NORA MAY FRENCH (1881-1907) was born in Aurora, New York, and moved to California when she was seven. Later, having become part of the literary circle surrounding George Sterling, she moved to live with him and his wife in Carmel-by-the-Sea, where she killed herself with cyanide. Though examples of her verse appeared in various periodicals in her lifetime, it was only after her death that her work was assembled in the volume *Poems* (1910), from which both "Vivisection" and "Rebuke" have been taken. "The Panther Woman" written in 1906 and unpublished in her lifetime, was not part of that collection.

NORMAN GALE (1862-1942), a native of Surrey, whom Richard Le Galliene called "a six-foot-three nightingale" was a contributor to *The Yellow Book* the author of numerous publications, including novels and volumes of poetry, such as *A Book of Quatrains* (1909) from which "The Sweater," "The Mouse" and "Right Royal" are taken. "Bees" originally appeared in the May 1894 issue of *The Artist*, the first issue of that magazine to come out after editorship had been taken away from Charles Kains Jackson—though the poem might well have been accepted by Jackson prior to his removal.

RICHARD LE GALLIENNE (1866-1947), under the influence of Oscar Wilde, turned to writing, and over a long career, produced numerous volumes, of both poetry and prose. A member of the Rhymers' Club and a frequent contributor to *The Yellow Book*, he played an important role in the "decadent" scene of the period. "The Décadent to His Soul" is taken from *English Poems* (1892).

JOHN GRAY (1866-1934), a more than close friend of Oscar Wilde and Marc-Andre Raffalovich, was a Catholic convert and an important member of the aesthetic circles of the 1890s. His first collection of verse, *Silverpoints* (1893), from which "Complaint," "Summer Past," and "Poem" are taken, consisted of original poetry and translations of Verlaine, Baudelaire, Mallarmé, and Rimbaud.

ALTHEA GYLES (186 -1949), was a poet and artist, whose illustrations adorned books by the likes of Oscar Wilde and Ernest Dowson. A lover of both Aleister Crowley, who called her the "wickedest man in the world", and the "decadent" publisher Leonard Smithers, she was a member of Hermetic Order of the Golden Dawn, before proceeding down other paths. Her illustrations and verse appeared in numerous magazines, such as the *Saturday Review, Kensington*, and the theosophical magazine *Orpheus*. "Sympathy" first appeared in the magazine *The Dome*, in 1897; "From Rosamor Dead to Favonius for whom She Died" first appeared in the December 1, 1906 issue of *The Academy*.

SADAKICHI HARTMANN (1867-1944), a writer and artist, was born on the artificial island of Dejima, Nagasaki, to a Japanese mother and German father. He was raised in Germany and in 1882 immigrated to the United States, where he led a Bohemian existence. He was arrested in 1893, due to the outrageous nature of his symbolist play Christ, and upon his release fled to Paris where he became friends with Verlaine and Mallarmé. Two of his self-published books he was unable to pay for upon their being printed, and so they were never released and instead sold by weight by the printer. "As the Lindens Shiver in Autumn Dreams" is taken from the self-published collection *Drifting Flowers of the Sea and Other Poems* (1904).

"LAURENCE HOPE" was the pseudonym of Violet Nicolson (1865-1904). She was brought up in England, but, at the age of sixteen, went to join her father in India where he was employed by the British Army as the editor of *The Civil and Military Gazette*. Her sisters were also both writers, one Annie Sophie Cory, wrote novels under the pseudonym of "Victoria Cross," while the other, Isabell Tate, edited the *Sind Gazette*. In 1889 Violet married the much older Colonel Malcolm Hassels Nicolson, notorious for his bravery and eccentricity. At one point, disguised as a boy and going to join her husband on the North West Frontier, her horse was taken by a brigand while she was on it, and she managed to kill the man with his own dagger. In 1901 she published *The Garden of Kama and Other Love Lyrics from India*, which presented her poetry as translations. The book became extremely popular, going through at least five editions in her lifetime. Two month's after her husband's death, she committed suicide with poison. "Malaria" and "To the Unattainable" are taken from *The Garden of Kama and Other Love Lyrics from India*; "Opium: Li's Riverside Hut at Taku" is taken from *Stars of the Desert* (1903).

GEORGE IVES (1867-1950), the illegitimate son of an English army officer, was born in Germany but raised by his grandmother in England and France and educated at Cambridge. He was the founder of the Order of Chaeronea, a secret homosexual society to which many notable British writers belonged, and was also one of the founding members of the British Society for the Study of Sex Psychology. He was, furthermore, the model for which the gentleman thief Raffles was based on. He wrote numerous volumes dealing with the subjects of criminology and sexology, as well as two volumes of verse. "I Can Trust Thee" and "Young God of Love" are taken from *Eros' Throne* (1900), while "To Slander" is taken from *Book of Chains* (1897).

CHARLES KAINS JACKSON (1857-1933) was, from 1888-1894, editor of the monthly art and design periodical *The Artist and Journal of Home Culture*, lending it a homosexual undercurrent for which it became known. Aside from being an associate of Frederick Rolfe, Lord Alfred Douglas, and John Addington Symonds, he was also a member of the Order of Chaeronea, the secret homosexual society which brought him into contact with George Ives and Montague Summers. The three "Impressions" in the current volume all first appeared in the March 10, 1893 issue of *The Spirit Lamp*, while "Lysis Aged XIII" is from the privately printed *Lysis (aet. xiii. xiv. xv.): a memory* (1924).

EDMUND JOHN (1883-1917) fought in the First World War, but was invalided in 1916. The following year he died of a drug overdose in Taormina, Sicily. The author of some of the most striking Decadent verse in the English language, his work is contained in three highly distinctive volumes, *The Flute of Sardonyx* (1913), from which both "Songe d'Ennui" and "Nocturne" have been taken, *The Wind in the Temple* (1915), from which "Litany of the Seven Devils" has been taken, and the posthumously published *Symphonie Symbolique* (1919).

LIONEL JOHNSON (1867-1902), a member of the Rhymers' Club, pursued a literary career in London, publishing work in various periodicals and also publishing an important study of Thomas Hardy. He slept during the day and stayed awake throughout the night. An alcoholic, he died after falling off a pub stool. "Vinum Daemonum" is taken from *Ireland: with Other Poems* (1897), while "The Age of a Dream" is from *Poems* (1895).

MAY KENDALL (1861-1943) was an English author who, though best known today for her collaboration with Andrew Lang on the novel *That Very Mab* (1885), was a highly gifted poet, her work in that regard being published in a number of journals of the day, and summarized in her two volumes of verse, *Dreams to Sell* (1887) and *Songs from Dreamland* (1894), the latter collection being the source of all four pieces in the current anthology.

ROBINSON KAY LEATHER (1864-1895), scholar, man of letters and chess player, was the editor of the undergraduate magazine at the University College at Liverpool, before spending time in Algiers in the hopes of curing the progressive paralysis which eventually killed him. He was good friends with Richard Le Galliene, with whom he published a book of short stories titled *The Student and the Body Snatcher and Other Trifles* (1890), and Norman Gale, with whom he published a book of poetry titled *On Two Strings* (1894). "Bubbles" is taken from *Verses* (1891).

EUGENE LEE-HAMILTON (1845-1907), the half-brother of Violet Paget, the writer whose pseudonym was "Vernon Lee," though born in London, spent much of his life on the Continent, most especially in Italy. Becoming paralyzed in 1873, he took up poetry in part as a distraction from his pain, dictating his poems and other literary works, which eventually ran to a dozen volumes, and included the great decadent novel *The Lord of the Dark Red Star* (1903). "Strangled" is taken from *Apollo and Marsyas and Other Poems* (1884); "Leonardo de Vinci to His Snakes" is taken from *Imaginary Sonnets* (1888); "Song of the Arrow-Poisoners" is taken from *The Fountain Youth* (1891); "Baudelaire" is taken from *Sonnets of the Wingless Hours* (1894).

EDWARD CRACROFT LEFROY (1855-1891), a clergyman known for haunting cricket and football matches and hanging out with athletes, shifted his literary allegiances between sermons and poetry that tended to be of a more heretical nature. He published *Windows of the Church and Other Sonnets* (1883), from which "Dream-Travel" is taken, *Cytisus and Galingale* (1883), and *Echoes from Theocritus* (1891) from which "Quem Di Diligunt" and "A Football Player" are taken. "Colores" is taken from *Edward Cracroft Lefroy, His Life and Poems* (1897), though it might have appeared elsewhere previously.

AMY LEVY (1861-1889), who began writing poetry in her teenage years, was the first Jewish woman at Cambridge University. In 1881 her first collection, *Xantippe and Other Verse*, from which "Felo de Se" is taken, was published, and in 1884, her second, *A Minor Poet and Other Verse*, from which "Sinfonia Eroica" is taken. Oscar Wilde, while editing the magazine *Woman's World*, received an unsolicited story from her which he accepted, and afterwards, impressed by her talents, commissioned a second story, two poems and two articles. Two of her novels *The Romance of a Shop* and *Reuben Sachs* appeared in 1888; she died by suicide the following year, at the age of 27. Just before her death she had been working on the proofs of *A London Plane-Tree and Other Verse* (1889), from which "To Vernon Lee" is taken.

ARTHUR MACHEN (1863-1947) was a Welsh author best known for his works of supernatural fiction, such as *The Great God Pan* (1894), *The Three Impostors* (1895), and *The White People* (1904). He is widely considered to be one of the greatest writers of horror fiction in the English language. "The Praise of Myfanwy" first appeared in the November 23, 1907 issue of *The Academy*.

GASCOIGNE MACKIE (1867-1952), whose early work was admired by John Addington Symonds, who at the same time called it "crude and young and yeasty," was the author of a number of books of verse, including *Charmides and Other Poems* (1898), *The Man of Kerioth and Other Poems* (1901), and *Andrea and Other Poems* (1908), the latter volume being that from which "At Clapham Junction" is taken.

THEO MARZIALS (1850-1920), born Théophile-Jules-Henri Marzials, aside from being a writer, was also a singer and composer, putting to music the words of both Christina Rosetti and Algernon Charles Swinburne. Possessed of a fine baritone voice, he wrote numerous lyrics, one of which, "Twickenham Ferry," is still remembered. Called, amongst other things, an eccentric, he was addicted to Chlorodyne, the principal ingredient of which was laudanum. A few of his poems appeared in *The Yellow Book*, but the only volume of verse he published was *The Gallery of Pigeons and Other Poems*, from which both "Châtelard" and "A Tragedy" are taken.

ADAH ISAACS MENKEN (1835-1868) was one of the most famous and highly paid American actresses of her day. Though there are many stories about her origins, it is generally agreed that she was the daughter of Auguste Théodore, a free Black man, and Marie, a Creole. While performing in Paris, in 1866, she was said to have had an affair with Alexandre Dumas père. Around this time, she sent a manuscript of her poetry to Algernon Charles Swinburne, and shortly thereafter a romance between the two began. Her single collection of poems, *Infelicia*, from which "Infelix" is taken, was published just subsequent to her death. Due to the fact that the book began with an unattributed quote from Swinburne, and possibly some stylistic similarities, some at the time speculated that he was, in fact, the author—which was, certainly, untrue.

STUART MERRILL (1863-1915) was born in Hampsead, New York, but spent most of his life in France and wrote the majority of his poetry in the French language. In1890 he published *Pastels in Prose*, a collection of his translations of French prose poems, which introduced many important symbolist writers, such as Éphraïm Mikhaël and Henri de Régnier, to English language readers. "The Chinese Lover's Ballad" first appeared in *Munsey's Magazine* in 1892; "Ballade of the Outcasts" first appeared in *The Nationalist* in 1889.

"G. F. MONKSHOOD" (1872-1910), the pseudonym of William James Clarke, was the translator of numerous works from the French, including books by Paul Bourget, Gustave Flaubert, Théophile Gautier, and Edmond de Goncourt. Amongst various other projects, he co-wrote *Algernon Charles Swinburne: A Study* (1901) with his friend Theodore Wratislaw, to whom he also dedicated his sole volume of poetry, *Nightshades* (1899), from which "Léonie" is taken.

GEORGE MOORE (1852-1933), though primarily re-membered for his Naturalist fiction, began his career with *Flowers of Passion*, a volume of morally exotic verse which he issued at his own expense in 1878, after being exposed in Paris to the work of Baudelaire, Mallarmé, and Catulle Mendès. After reading a review in which it was written that the book "should be burned by the common hangman while the author is being whipped at the cart's tail," Moore withdrew the book from circulation, but unable to lay low for too long, three years later, came out with a second volume in a similar vein titled *Pagan Poems*. "A Sapphic Dream" and "The Corpse" are both taken from *Flowers of Passion*, while "Chez Mois" is taken from *Pagan Poems*.

SAROJINI NAIDU (1879-1949) was an Indian political activist and poet who received part of her education in England. "Eastern Dancers" originally appeared in the September 1896 issue of *The Savoy*, and was later reprinted in her first book of poetry *The Golden Threshold* (1905), which also contained an introduction by Arthur Symons.

VICTOR BENJAMIN NEUBURG (1883-1940) was an English poet who became closely aligned with Aleister Crowley, who initiated him into his magical organization the A∴A∴, and would later say that Neuburg "produced some of the finest poetry of which the English language can boast." "The Cauldron" originally appeared in the February 1909 issue of *The Theosophical Review*, and was reprinted in *The Triumph of Pan* (1910), a collection published by Crowley's The Equinox press.

PERCY OSBORN (1870-1951) published two books in his lifetime, both of which were translations and adaptations from the Greek, the first being *Rose Leaves from Philostratus* (1901), and the second *The Poems of Sappho* (1909). During the early 1890s, under the byline of "P.L.O.," his work appeared frequently in *The Spirit Lamp*, the September 17, 1893 issue of which contained "Heartsease and Orchid," though the poem was written in December 1892.

WILLIAM THEODORE PETERS (1862-1904) was an eccentric American writer and actor, who spent a large portion of his life in Paris, where he was one of the very few who attended Oscar Wilde's funeral. He was a friend of Ernest Dowson's, who wrote a poem dedicated to him and his Renaissance cloak. Peters further commissioned Dowson to write the play *The Pierrot of the Minute*, for him to act in. He contributed to many of the journals of his day, mostly clever quatrains, and published a few children's books, and the volume of verse *Posies Out of Rings, and Other Conceits* (1896) from which all the pieces in the current volume are taken.

PERCY EDWARD PINKERTON (1855-1946) was, along with Ernest Dowson, Havelock Ellis, Arthur Symons, Victor Plarr and Alexander Teixeira de Mattos, a member of the Lutetian Society, whose aim was the issuing of un-expurgated translations of the novels of Émile Zola. Aside from Zola's works, Pinkerton translated numerous books from the Russian, German and Italian, as well as producing several volumes of verse. "Auto-da-Fé" and "Mors Pronuba" are taken from the *Adriatica* (1894), while "The Shrine" is from *At Hazbero' and Other Poems* (1909).

DOLLIE RADFORD, (née Caroline Maitland; 1858-1920), was one of the most highly regarded poets of her day. A close friend of Eleanor Marx, she became a regular at the Marx household, and published her first poem in

Progress: A Monthly Magazine of Advanced Thought in 1883, the same year that she married the poet Ernest Radford. She contributed to many of the periodicals of the day, including *The Yellow Book*, and published numerous volumes of both poetry and prose. "A Novice" is taken from *Songs and Other Verses* (1895).

MARC-ANDRÉ RAFFALOVICH (1864-1934) was born in Paris to a wealthy Jewish family who had immigrated from Odessa the year before. He studied in Oxford, and then moved to London, where he hosted a well-known solon, became the lover of John Gray, and converted to Catholicism. He wrote six volumes of poetry in English and, in French, a great deal of work on the subject of homosexuality, most importantly *Uranisme et unisexualité: étude sur différentes manifestations de l'instinct sexuel* (1896). "Stramony" and "On the Borderland of Sin" are taken from *Tuberose and Meadowsweet* (1895); "Blue and Orange", "Love, Vice, Crime, and Sin" and "The Green Carnation" are taken from *The Thread and the Path* (1895).

FREDERICK ROLFE, a.k.a. Baron Corvo (1860-1913), was born in Cheapside, London. In 1886, he converted to Roman Catholicism. His short stories were published in various periodicals, including *The Yellow Book*. He wrote *A History of the Borgias* (1901), as well as a number of novels, the most famous of them being *Hadrian the Seventh* (1904). He died in poverty in Venice. "Sonnet (After the manner of C.J.R. Esquire): Of Gore" was originally published anonymously in the March 14, 1891 issue of *The Anti-Jacobin*, while "Sonnet: A Victim" first appeared in the July 31, 1897 issue of *The Holywell Record*.

EDGAR SALTUS (1855-1921), the half-brother of Francis Saltus Saltus, was one of the most important American Decadent writers, composing, in glittering prose, volumes of both fiction and non-fiction, including *Imperial Purple* (1892) and *Oscar Wilde: An Idler's Impression* (1917). Though his output as a poet was relatively modest, those he did write carried with them the heady incense of his aesthetic. "Akosmism" first appeared in the June 1888 issue of *Belford's Magazine*; "Imeros" was first published in the December 1888 issue of *Lippincott's Monthly Magazine*; "Poppies and Mandragora" is taken from the collection of the same name published posthumously in 1926, though the poem itself was written in New York in 1912.

FRANCIS SALTUS SALTUS (1849-1889), the half-brother of Edgar Saltus, was born in New York City, but is said to have spent a large part of his life in Paris, where he was a protégé of Théophile Gautier. A great bohemian and drinker of absinthe, he was part of a group of writers who converged in Billy Moulds' bar in Manhattan. Though he was a prolific author, writing for various periodicals under his own name and pseudonyms, he only published a single volume of verse during his lifetime, *Honey and Gall* (1873), from which both "Spleen" and "Souls of Flowers" were taken, while "Vulnerable" is from the posthumously published collection *Shadows and Ideals* (1890).

CHARLES SAYLE (1864-1924) was an English bibliographer and librarian and the author of a number of works, including the play *Wicliff* (1887), and several volumes of verse. He was a friend and correspondent with many notable figures, including Lionel Johnson and Oscar Wilde. He worked for a good while on a biography of Frederick Rolfe, but ended up letting A. J. A. Symons use his material for his own *Quest for Corvo*. "Poenitentia" is taken from *Musa Consolatrix* (1893).

WILLIAM SHARP (1855-1905) was a Scottish writer who also wrote under the pseudonym of "Fiona Macleod," producing under this dual personality numerous studies, novels, and volumes of poetry. A member of the Hermetic Order of the Golden Dawn, a forceful part of the Celtic revival, and a translator of a number of Belgian Symbolist writers, Sharp's multi-faceted character made him a difficult author to easily define. "A Paris Nocturne" was originally published in the New York *Independent,* in 1890; "An Untold Story" was originally published in 1892, under the pseudonym of "Lionel Wingrave," in the single issue of the *Pagan Review*, the entire contents of which were written by Sharp under various pseudonyms.

DORA SIGERSON SHORTER (1866-1918) was born in Dublin to the author and physician George Singerson and the author Hester Varian, and was the wife of the journalist Clement Shorter. A sculptor of note and an important part of the Irish Literary Revival, she was the author of a number of volumes of both prose and poetry, including *The Fairy Changeling and Other Poems* (1898), from which "Beware" is taken.

"ALAN STANLEY" (1871-1951) was the pseudonym employed by the clergyman Stanley Addleshaw for much of his poetry. Using his own name, he contributed to various publications, including *The Gentleman's Magazine* and *The Spirit Lamp*, offering assessments of such authors as Walter Pater and Arthur Symons, but it was under his pseudonym that he published his underground classic *Love Lyrics* (1894), from which both "Now Dies the Sun" and "A Night Club and a Valse" are taken.

COUNT ERIC STENBOCK (1860-1895), the stylized name of Stanislaus Eric Stenbock, Count of Bogesund, was born in South West England to Lucy Sophia Frerichs, an English cotton heiress, and Count Erich Stenbock, who was of a distinguished Swedish noble family of the Baltic German House of nobility in Reval. He inherited his family's estates in 1885 and returned to live in his manor house at Kolkbriefly for a period before returning to England. In his life he published three volumes of poetry and one collection of short stories, *Studies of Death* (1894). He died as a result of alcoholism and opium addiction. "The Song of the Unwept Tear" is taken from *Love, Sleep & Dreams* (1881); "The Lunatic Lover" is taken from *Myrtle, Rue, and Cypress* (1883); "The Death-Watch" is taken from *The Shadow of Death* (1893).

MONTAGUE SUMMERS (1880-1948) was an English occultist, poet and man of letters. His most famous products were a series of colorful studies of vampirism, lycanthropy and witchcraft, such as *The History of Witchcraft and Demonology* (1926) and *The Vampire: His Kith and Kin* (1928), as well as several volumes of supernatural stories which he edited. His posthumously published novella *The Bride of Christ* shows evidence of his dabbling in Decadence, as does "To a Dead Acolyte" which is taken from *Antinous and Other Poems* (1907).

GEORGE STERLING (1869-1926) was born in Sag Harbor, New York, but at the age of 19 went to California, establishing himself in the Bay Area, and later in Carmel-by-the-Sea. His first book of poetry, *The Testimony of the Sun and Other Poems* (1903), garnered him much praise from the Bay Area Bohemians, but it was his poem "A Wine of Wizardry" which brought him into the national spotlight when it was published in *Cosmopolitan* magazine in 1907, accompanied by a prefatory article by the already famous Ambrose Bierce declaring Sterling to be "a very great poet—incomparably the greatest we have on this side of the Atlantic." Sterling, for many years, carried with him a bottle of cyanide, which he finally used at the Bohemian Club in San Francisco, when H.L. Mencken failed to arrive for an appointed meeting. "A Mood" is taken from *A Wine of Wizardry and Other Poems* (1909).

VINCENT O'SULLIVAN (1868-1940) was born in New York City, but spent much of his life in England and France, where he became friends with many of the Decadent figures of the day, such as Aubrey Beardsley, who provided the frontispiece to his volume of short stories *A Book of Bargains* (1896) as well as the cover for his volume of poetry *The house of Sin* (1897), and Oscar Wilde, whom he helped support when the latter was released from Reading Gaol. A master of the macabre short story and the Decadent English poem, Vincent O'Sullivan died in Paris in poverty and was buried in a common grave. "Malaria," "Drug," and "Shadows" are all taken from *The House of Sin*.

ALGERNON CHARLES SWINBURNE (1837-1909) was one of the greatest of English poets and a prototypical figure of the English Decadent Movement. Oscar Wild said that he was "a braggart in matters of vice, who had done everything he could to convince his fellow citizens of his homosexuality and bestiality without being in the slightest degree a homosexual or a bestializer." At the age of 42, suffering ill health due to acute alcoholism and other excesses, he was taken in by his friend Theodore Watts-Dunton. His constitution being greatly restored due to a more "wholesome" lifestyle, he continued to write, producing numerous volumes of criticism and verse, though some said his best work was from his earlier days. He died of influenza in 1909. "Satia te Sanguine" is taken from *Poems and Ballads* (1866).

JOHN ADDINGTON SYMONDS (1840-1893), though married and the father of four daughters, managed to cultivate a reputation as a man interested in *l'amour de l'impossible*, due to both real-life affairs and his writings, which include *A Problem in Greek Ethics* (1873), and numerous homosexually slanted amorous poems. "A Portrait" and "Wo Die Götter Night Sind, Walten Gespenster" are both taken from *Vagabunduli Libellus* (1884); "Love in Dreams" is from *New and Old: A Volume of Verse* (1880).

ARTHUR SYMONS (1865-1945), one of the leading exponents of Decadent literature in the English speaking world, was co-editor of *The Savoy*, and author of numerous works, including *The Symbolist Movement in Literature* (1899). He translated books by a number of important writers, including Gabriele D'Annunzio and Villiers de l'Isle Adam. "Bianca" is taken from his collection *London Nights* (1897); "The Absinthe Drinker" and "Morbidezza" are from *Silhouettes* (1896).

VANCE THOMPSON (1863-1925) was an American literary critic, novelist, poet and low-carbohydrate diet writer. A good friend of James Huneker, with whom he edited the Symbolist leaning periodical *M'lle New York,* he also published, among a great many other things, *French Portraits* (1900), which contained chapters on such writers as Catulle Mendès, Jean Richepin, and Marcel Schwob. "The Night Watchman" and "Daybreak" are both taken from *Verse: The Night Watchman and Other Poems* (1915).

JOHN TODHUNTER (1839-1916) was born in Dublin. A member of the Rhymers' Club, whose members included Lionel Johnson and Ernest Dowson, he was responsible for numerous volumes of verse and several plays. "Euthanasia" first appeared in the anthology, *The Second Book of the Rhymers' Club* (1894).

SANDYS WASON (1867-1950), was the founder and, along with Lord Alfred Douglas, editor of *The Spirit Lamp,* the magazine from which "Kabale und Liebe" is taken, the same item later appearing in *Magenta Minutes: Nonsense Verse* (1913). He published several other books, including the science fiction novel *Palafox* (1927), and became a cleric of the Church of England, receiving a post in Cornwall, from which he was removed for "doctrinal and liturgical disobedience."

ROSAMUND MARRIOTT WATSON (née Ball; 1860-1911) was an English writer who began her career publishing articles and poems under the pseudonyms "Rushworth Armytage" and "Graham R. Tomson," the first of which was connected to her marriage to her first husband George Francis Armytage, and the second to the artist Arthur Tomson, her second husband. She later divorced Tomson and lived for the rest of her life with the writer H. B. Marriott Watson. She was the editor of the women's magazine *Sylvia's Journal*, as well as a contributor to *The Yellow Book*, and many other periodicals. Ten volumes of her work were published in her lifetime, seven of them being verse. "Walpurgis" is taken from *Vespertilia and Other Verses* (1895), while "The Golden Touch" is from *After Sunset* (1904).

HELEN HAY WHITNEY (1875-1944), the daughter of two prominent American families and subsequently marrying into the wealthy Whitney family, was, in the earlier part of her career, a poet of some note, publishing verse in, among other places, *Harper's Magazine*, *The Critic* and *The Metropolitan Magazine*. She published a number of books, including several for children. "A Dream in Fever" is taken from *Some Verses* (1898); "The Forgiveness," "Flowers of Ice" and "To a Moth" are taken from *Sonnets and Songs* (1905); "The Monk in His Garden" is taken from *Gypsy Verses* (1907); "An Impressionist Picture" is taken from *Herbs and Apples* (1910).

OSCAR WILDE (1854-1900), one of the leading figures of the English Decadent Movement, though principally known for his plays and fiction, began his career as a poet, with *Ravenna* in 1878, followed by *Poems* in 1881. The three poems in the current volume were uncollected during the author's lifetime, but their publication data is as follows: "The Harlot's House" first appeared in The Dramatic Review in 1885; "Un Amant De Nos Jours" (which is an earlier version of the poem titled "The New Remorse") originally appeared in *The Court and Society Review* in 1887; "Symphony in Yellow" first appeared in Centennial Magazine in 1889.

THEODORE WRATISLAW (1871-1933), one of the quintessential minor decadent poets of the English language, published a few slim volumes during the 1890s before work as a solicitor seems to have swallowed up those impulses. "After Death" is taken from *Love's Memorial* (1892), "In the Ball-room" is taken from *Caprices* (1893), and "Sonnet Macabre," "White Lilies" and "Hothouse Flowers" are all taken from *Orchids* (1896).

A PARTIAL LIST OF SNUGGLY BOOKS

MAY ARMAND BLANC *The Last Rendezvous*
G. ALBERT AURIER *Elsewhere and Other Stories*
CHARLES BARBARA *My Lunatic Asylum*
S. HENRY BERTHOUD *Misanthropic Tales*
LÉON BLOY *The Tarantulas' Parlor and Other Unkind Tales*
ÉLÉMIR BOURGES *The Twilight of the Gods*
CYRIEL BUYSSE *The Aunts*
JAMES CHAMPAGNE *Harlem Smoke*
FÉLICIEN CHAMPSAUR *The Latin Orgy*
BRENDAN CONNELL *Metrophilias*
BRENDAN CONNELL *Unofficial History of Pi Wei*
RAFAELA CONTRERAS *The Turquoise Ring and Other Stories*
DANIEL CORRICK (editor)
    Ghosts and Robbers: An Anthology of German Gothic Fiction
ADOLFO COUVE *When I Think of My Missing Head*
QUENTIN S. CRISP *Aiaigasa*
ALADY DILKE *The Outcast Spirit and Other Stories*
CATHERINE DOUSTEYSSIER-KHOZE *The Beauty of the Death Cap*
ÉDOUARD DUJARDIN *Hauntings*
BERIT ELLINGSEN *Now We Can See the Moon*
ERCKMANN-CHATRIAN *A Malediction*
ALPHONSE ESQUIROS *The Enchanted Castle*
ENRIQUE GÓMEZ CARRILLO *Sentimental Stories*
DELPHI FABRICE *Flowers of Ether*
DELPHI FABRICE *The Red Spider*
BENJAMIN GASTINEAU *The Reign of Satan*
EDMOND AND JULES DE GONCOURT *Manette Salomon*
REMY DE GOURMONT *From a Faraway Land*
REMY DE GOURMONT *Morose Vignettes*
GUIDO GOZZANO *Alcina and Other Stories*
GUSTAVE GUICHES *The Modesty of Sodom*
EDWARD HERON-ALLEN *The Complete Shorter Fiction*
EDWARD HERON-ALLEN *Three Ghost-Written Novels*
RHYS HUGHES *Cloud Farming in Wales*
J.-K. HUYSMANS *The Crowds of Lourdes*
J.-K. HUYSMANS *Knapsacks*
COLIN INSOLE *Valerie and Other Stories*
JUSTIN ISIS *Pleasant Tales II*

CPSIA information can be obtained
at www.ICGtesting.com
Printed in the USA
LVHW102303150422
716321LV00004B/233

Enjoy
Shirley McCormick

Ham, Lamb, Ram, Bull, Beef, and Bear

The Humor in a Lifetime of Medical Practice

J. Judson Booker, III, M.D.

PublishAmerica
Baltimore

First printing

ISBN: 1-60672-627-7
PUBLISHED BY PUBLISHAMERICA, LLLP
www.publishamerica.com
Baltimore

Printed in the United States of America